the EDIBLE MEXICAN GARDEN

Rosalind Creasy

PERIPLUS

First published in 2000 by
PERIPLUS EDITIONS (HK) LTD.,
with editorial offices at 153 Milk Street,
Boston, Massachusetts 02109 and
5 Little Road #08-01
Singapore 536983.

Library of Congress Cataloging-in-Publication Data is available.

ISBN 962-593-297-6

Distributed by

USA
Tuttle Publishing
Distribution Center
364 Airport Industrial Park
North Clarendon, VT 05759-9436
Tel: (802) 773-8930
Tel: (800) 526-2778

SOUTHEAST ASIA
Berkeley Books Pte. Ltd.
5 Little Road #08-01
Singapore 536983
Tel: (65) 280-3320
Fax: (65) 280-6290

CANADA
Raincoast Books
8680 Cambie Street
Vancouver, Canada V6P 6M9
Tel: (604) 323-7100
Fax: (604) 323-2600

JAPAN
Tuttle Publishing
RK Building, 2nd Floor
2-13-10 Shimo-Meguro
Meguro-ku
Tokyo 153-0064
Tel: (03) 5437-0171
Fax: (03) 5437-0755

First edition
05 04 03 02 01 00
10 9 8 7 6 5 4 3 2 1

Design by Kathryn Sky-Peck

PRINTED IN SINGAPORE

contents

edible
mexican
gardens

My husband and I moved from the Boston area to Northern California in 1967. For a few days I was homesick and needed a reason to feel we had made the right decision. A former Bostonian friend had settled here a few years earlier and she invited us over for supper. Well, sir— she served tacos with homemade salsa. What a revelation! I'd never tasted anything so good—I was hooked. A few more Mexican meals and a trip to San Francisco and I knew I had found my spot in the sun.

Looking back, it's amazing to me to see how, over the years, my day-to-day Yankee cooking has completely changed. Grilled cheese sandwiches somehow turned into quesadillas, my bread box always has tortillas, a *comal*

(flat Mexican griddle) sits on the stove, ever ready to toast herbs or grill an onion, and chiles show up in so many of my meals that when members of my tender-tongued East Coast family come to visit, I have to change my whole repertoire.

My garden, too, reflects the south-of-the-border shift. Numerous trips to Mexico and much time spent in the Southwest, where Mexican culture dominates, not only changed many of the crops I grow but my garden aesthetic as well. As a landscape designer, I can design an English garden with the best of them—good enough, in fact, that on occasion I've had home-

sick Brits stand at the end of my walk and weep for home—but despite my English blood, my heart's not in it. I keep coming back to an in-your-face, colorful garden style, all tangled with flowering vines and squash and filled with chiles and dahlias.

The gardens and recipes that I share with you in the following pages are from my years of experience, much of it from muddling through and still more learned from generous gardeners and cooks. I hope you find the information zestful, inspirational, and even more exciting in that the vegetables and herbs, and the cooking methods, are based in the Americas. I thoroughly enjoy Chinese and Italian vegetables, Southeast Asian herbs, and I glory in French cooking techniques, but over the years I find that growing and roasting great tomatoes and chiles, hominying corn, and stewing beans brings me truly home.

how to grow a mexican garden

Most of the vegetables in a Mexican garden are grown in a routine manner. The tomatoes, onions, hot peppers, and squash, for instance, are often the very same as or similar to those we usually grow in the United States.

Mexico is a huge country whose many climates range from tropical to temperate. Most gardeners in the United States can grow a good number of Mexico's vegetables and herbs, but the nearer one lives to the Mexican border, the more options there will be for growing specific Mexican varieties.

Let's start by surveying options open to gardeners in Canada and the northern U.S. They can grow numerous varieties of common vegetables used in Mexican cooking, such as tomatoes, Swiss chard, lettuce, radishes, white onions, and snap beans. They can also choose vegetables less common in the States but characteristic of Mexican cooking, such as many kinds of dry beans; some of the dent corns; jalapeños; purslane; tomatillos; round, light-colored zucchini-type squash, and the important herbs cilantro and epazote. Nurseries with a good selection of appropriate varieties for these short-season areas are Johnny's Selected Seeds, Nichols Garden Seeds, Stokes Seeds, and Abundant Life Seed Foundation.

For more southerly gardeners, the array of authentic Mexican varieties is larger. Because the fall stays warm longer, they can grow day-length-sensitive varieties (varieties that don't set fruit until the days get short in early fall) of winter squash and Mexican corn. There are also more chile options, plus the tender perennials, such as jícama and chayote, which need a long, warm growing season and a mild winter.

To obtain seeds of Mexican vegetables and herbs, consult the seed companies given in the Resources section of the book. Mexican seed companies are not cited, as they carry mostly commercial varieties of standard vegetables common in this country. Seeds of varieties favored by Mexican gardeners in the States can sometimes be purchased from seed racks in local Mexican grocery stores, especially in the spring. The rest of the varieties, including unusual Mexican herbs, are available from specialty mail-order nurseries or from local nurseries located in the Southwest.

In Mexico, most gardeners obtain their seeds from local purveyors, and if they are open-pollinated varieties, not hybrids, they keep the seeds from their plants from year to year.

Once you obtain your Mexican varieties, you may want to save your seeds too. See the sidebar entitled Saving Seeds for basic information. For specific information on saving the seeds of beans, corn, peppers, and tomatoes, see the "Encyclopedia of Mexican Vegetables."

You will most probably get most of the seeds you want from the specialty seed companies listed in the Resources section but, if you visit Mexico, you can shop in the markets for an even larger selection. Most vegetable seeds in commercial packaging are OK to bring back home, except Mexican

Seeds of Mexican varieties *(opposite, left)* are sold in many Mexican markets in North America. They are generally available only in the spring. Large blue buckets in a Yucatán market *(opposite, right)* offers a variety of seeds and spices. The harvest from one of my many Mexican gardens includes tomatoes, corn, chilis, and pumpkin *(opposite, below)*.

[Saving Seeds]

I find saving seeds simple and satisfying process. The following general guidelines apply no matter what kind of seeds you are saving. See the "Encyclopedia of Mexican Vegetables" for more specific information on saving the seeds of beans, corn, peppers, squash, and tomatoes. In addition, everyone interested in seed saving will benefit from reading *Seed to Seed,* by Suzanne Ashworth. She gives detailed instructions on how to save seeds of all kinds of vegetables.

1. Save seed from open-pollinated (nonhybrid) plants only. Saving vegetable seeds from hybrids is wasted energy, as they will not come true—in other words, there's no telling what you will get. Hybrids are created by crossing two vegetable variety parents; a gardener needs to know which two parents are crossed to create an identical variety. For proprietary reasons, seed companies keep that information to themselves. They do however, label hybrids and F1 hybrids (first-generation hybrids) on their seed packages, so you know which are hybrids and which are open-pollinated.

2. When you are saving seeds to perpetuate a variety, you need to take steps to prevent cross-pollination. With some plants, such as beans, which are primarily self-pollinated, cross-pollination problems are few. For others, more protection is needed. Get to know the vegetable families, as members of the same family often cross-pollinate. A list of vegetable families is included in Appendix A with the information on crop rotation; see page 94.

3. Do not save seeds of diseased plants. Save only the finest fruits from the best plants of your favorite varieties. You need to learn to recognize diseases because some (particularly viruses) are transmitted in seeds.

4. Label your seed rows and seed containers; your memory will play tricks on you.

5. Never plant all your seeds at once, lest the elements wipe them out.

6. To maintain a strong gene pool, select seeds from a number of plants, not just one or two. (This does not apply to self-pollinating varieties.)

7. Only mature, ripe seeds are viable. Learn what such seeds look like for all your vegetables.

---

corn, which is confiscated at the border as illegal to bring into the United States. Another option is to visit a Mexican market near you to shop for seeds of pozole corn and dry beans. But when you grow these grocery store seeds out, be prepared to baby them for a few years. The folks I spoke with in the community garden in San José found it took two or three seasons to acclimatize the Mexican market corn, in particular, to their own gardens. Be aware, too, of the possibility that in wet, cold climates they may never acclimatize.

To get you started with your own Mexican garden, in the next section I rhapsodize about my own Mexican gardens, both full size and in containers, and Kit Anderson shares her Vermont Mexican garden as well. For specific information on each vegetable, see the "Encyclopedia of Mexican Vegetables."

Chayote, white onions, tomatoes, and chilis are the basis for many a great Mexican meal.

creasy
mexican
gardens

For three decades, I have been an active vegetable gardener, much of it professionally. In the first decade, I mastered the basics like sweet corn, tomatoes, snap beans and was ready for something more exotic. Inspired by my travels, I decided to try growing ethnic vegetables of all types; from Mexican amaranths and Italian radicchios to Asian pac chois, tucking them in among their more prosaic cousins. Eventually, armed with all my new knowledge. I started a large garden cookbook and decided to grow a number of ethnic theme gardens for the book, including a Mexican one. I needed to grow out many unusual vegetables and herbs to develop my recipes. Also, I wanted to see how prototypical ethnic gardens went together and how well they fit into a standard American garden.

My first Mexican garden was planted in the corner of my backyard nearly fifteen years ago. It included all sorts of vegetables and herbs I had never seen before, much less grown, including epazote, huauzontlí, grain amaranths, and wild chiles, plus numerous unusual varieties of familiar vegetables, including grinding corns, tomatoes, peppers, lima beans, and sunflowers and pumpkins, for their seeds.

I not only wanted the vegetables to be Mexican but, as a landscape designer and photographer, I wanted the garden to give the feel of Mexican home gardens I knew. The ones I was familiar with were filled with exuberance, joy, and colorful flowers—and, in most of Mexico, planted in layers, with vegetables, herbs, and flowers among and under fruiting and flowering trees.

With these design goals in mind, I added a number of flowers I associate with Mexico, namely, tithonia (also called Mexican sunflower), Mexican sage (*Salvia leucantha*) and two south-of-the-border favorites, marigolds and nasturtiums. Because Mexican peppers, tomatoes, and tomatillos need a long growing season, I seeded them in the house under lights, starting with the peppers in February. A month later, I started the tomatoes, and a few weeks after that, the tomatillos. Once they became mature enough, I moved them outside to my cold frame.

I must say, I mastered the exuberance component! The garden spilled out of its boundaries, thanks in part to my great organic soil, which caused the corn to grow to 14 feet, the amaranths to tower over the tomatoes, and the tomatillos to sprawl over everything. The joy was evident, too; it was so much fun to explore a whole new garden culture and cuisine. Tacos, refried beans, and hominy from red dent corn was great fun. The bright colors, though, were definitely missing. Even with the addition of impatiens and gloriosa daisies at midsummer, I thought the garden still a bit too pale.

A few years later, I set out to grow another Mexican garden, this time with lots of color! And I really went for it this time. I filled up the whole front yard. Bougainvilleas, dahlias, cannas, morning glories, marigolds, nasturtiums, and zinnias were sprinkled among the vegetable beds and along the front path. For a little more

North American gardeners need to start a number of Mexican specialties from seeds in order to get a jump on the season. Appendix A gives specific information for starting seeds inside. I use a cold frame *(opposite, above)* as intermediate housing for my tomatillos, jicama, chilis, tomatoes, and Mexican herbs I've started inside. As the weather warms, I gradually leave the lid open longer. About fifteen years ago, I planted my first Mexican garden and filled it with corn, pumpkins, tomatillos, lima beans, and sunflowers *(opposite, below)*. It was a greatly productive garden—but didn't have enough color for my taste.

oomph, I had a trellis painted with primary colors and topped with a sun face created by my artist friend, Marcy Hawthorne.

Well, let me tell you, it worked. This garden stopped joggers in their tracks. Here among the suburban lawns and polite evergreens was an in-your-face-garden so filled with color and flowers you could hardly see all the veggies. I'd found the formula!

Since that time, I've created numerous Mexican gardens, including two minigardens I filled with Mexican herbs and chiles in colorful containers and a large front garden of big running squash and bush beans with a

front border filled with sunflowers, scarlet runner beans, amaranths, and giant Mexican corn. This garden featured all plants from the New World and it was sensational.

My last Mexican garden was enclosed by a stucco wall and included a small patio of random paving stones interlaced with broken blue tiles. It was planted early, as soon as the weather warmed up in early April, with the tomatillo 'Toma Verde,' some Mexican chiles—poblano, jalapeño, serrano, 'Habañero,' 'Mulato,' and 'Chili de Arbol'—and 'Beefsteak' and 'Costoluco Genovese' tomatoes, all of which we had started from seeds and hardened off in the cold frame. We filled some of the room between the plants with 'Iceberg' lettuce and cilantro, knowing these would be long gone before the other plants filled out. Unfortunately, the weather got unusually cold; in fact, we had a record-cold April and May

A few years after my first Mexican garden, I planned one for the front yard *(above)*. This time I put in a bright-colored arbor and added lots of bright flowers like dahlias, sunflowers, marigolds, nasturtiums, and cannas. The large beds were filled with chilis, corn, pumpkins, squash, and tomatoes as well as epazote, Mexican tarragon, and Mexican oregano. This iteration was so splashy it stopped traffic! A harvest from one of my latest Mexican garden *(opposite)* includes white onions, lima beans, tomatoes, chard, corn, beans, and lots of chilis.

and needed to put red plastic mulch down around the tomatoes and chiles to keep them going. We delayed more planting as well. Consequently, the 'Golden Bantam' corn, 'Peruano' dry beans, chayote, jícama, watermelon, 'Grey Zucchini,' and grain amaranth, all of which need very warm conditions, didn't go in until early June. The warmth also brought on the purslane (pigweed), which we usually pull out right away. This time, though, we let it grow and fill out until it was big enough to harvest. What a revelation. I'd been pulling it out for years. It tasted so good in some of our recipes I'm sure I will keep some of it around indefinitely.

To fill out the garden, I sent away for Mexican specialties, including epazote, Mexican tarragon, cumin, huauzontlí, and chia, and grew most of them in containers. For bright colors, I planted lots of zinnias, petunias, and marigolds in cheery containers. I especially liked the hot pink and orange plastic buckets I had purchased in the Tijuana produce market.

I'm sure I will continue to create new Mexican gardens for years to come. They are so cheerful and exuberant, the neighbors love to look at them, and eating their bounty is one of our favorite family feasts.

My most recent Mexican garden has many containers filled with Mexican herbs and chilis. The corn and watermelons fill the back beds; tomatoes and peppers in the middle and driveway beds. Jícama rambles over the low front fence and a chayote wanders around behind the corn.

[*Flowers in the Mexican Garden*]

Flowers are integral to a Mexican garden and while they add lots of life and color, as an added benefit they attract hundreds of beneficial insects to help protect against pests. When I started growing Mexican-style gardens I put in too few flowers and the gardens never looked quite right, now I include many. I don't always stick to flowers from Mexico, using plants like gomphrena and impatiens, but I find that the varieties from that part of the world look the most at home.

Many of our most popular flowers originated in Mexico including: marigolds, zinnias, nasturtiums, morning glories, cosmos, tithonias, sunflowers, verbenas, and many different sages. Bougainvillea and cannas are two other plants, native to tropical South America, that look particularly at home in a Mexican garden.

When I choose my flower varieties I lean toward bright primary colors and include lots of orange and hot pinks. I plan out where the flowers go by determining their final height at maturity. That means I usually put the tall sunflower varieties and tithonias in the back of the border in among or in front of the corn and tall amaranths (choosing the north side of the garden so they won't shade the other plants). I use the full-size cosmos, tall zinnias and marigolds, and most sages in the middle of the border, often among tomatoes and tomatillos; and I interplant the dwarf marigolds and verbena among the peppers and herbs. Dwarf nasturtiums I use for the borders of beds and in containers, and the large vining ones I use to cascade out of planter boxes. Morning glories are great on arbors, sometimes interplanted with chayotes or jicama, and I like to cascade them over a fence.

A garden full of bright-colored flowers speaks to Mexico. As a bonus, it also gives you armloads of flowers to bring in the house for bouquets.

mini mexican herb gardens

I have many colorful containers of Mexican herbs decorating my garden, even though I live in a mild climate, USDA Zone 9. Part of the reason I plant them is that they look great and I can keep them near the kitchen, but mostly I grow them because my climate is too cold to overwinter most of them. My solution is to grow the tenderest of them in containers and then either put them in my cold frame or bring them inside to my windowsill.

The Mexican herbs I've tried in containers are: cilantro, culantro, epazote, Mexican oregano, hoja santa, spearmint, and Mexican tarragon.

I was not always successful at growing plants in containers; in fact, at first I lost most of them before winter even set in. Through trial and error, I've found what I call the secrets for growing herbs in containers:

1. I use only soil mixes formulated for containers. Garden soil drains poorly and pulls away from the sides of the container, allowing most of the water to run out, and it often is filled with weed seeds. Straight compost is too fine and plants will drown.

2. Containers must have drainage holes in the bottom to prevent the plant from drowning. At planting time, I cover the holes with a piece of window screening or small square of weed cloth to keep dirt in and slugs out. (New evidence indicates that gravel or pottery shards in the bottom actually interfere with drainage.)

One of my favorite patio designs included a chair from Mexico designed by Roberto Matias from Oaxaca. Around it I cluster containers of 'Super Chile,' a yellow ornamental pepper, a container of Mexican oregano, and a pepino plant native to South America. A tall chiltepín chili plant was very productive and by the holidays was covered with red fruits. I added marigolds, sunflowers, and some blue statice to give color.

3. I now use only containers large enough to provide generously for the plant's root system and hold enough soil to avoid constant watering. I find most herbs grow best in large containers 18 inches, or more, in diameter. My southern friends report that in their climate, large containers are mandatory because the roots on the south side of small pots bake in the hot sun.

4. After years of pale plants, I found I need to fertilize frequently and evenly. For me, biweekly doses of fish emulsion work well, as does granulated fish meal renewed every five or six weeks.

5. I find the most difficult aspect of container growing is to maintain the correct moisture in the soil. Cilantro and mint suffer if allowed to dry out, but the Mexican oregano, *Lippia graveolens,* is drought tolerant and succumbs to root rot when overwatered. When I learned how to water properly, I was on the road to success.

6. When I bring the herbs in for the winter, I give them a half day of shade for a few weeks to prepare them for darker conditions. Before bringing them in, I wash the foliage well. I then locate them in a bright, sunlit spot away from heater vents. I water them less indoors than when they are actively growing in the garden. I keep them barely moist and I fertilize only when the days get longer in the spring.

A further note on watering: All gardeners need to learn to water container plants properly. Even in rainy climates, hand watering containers is usually a necessity, as little rain penetrates the umbrella of foliage covering a pot. I find that it is most helpful to water the container at least twice—the first time to moisten the soil (I think of it as moistening a dry sponge.) and the rest to actually wet it. To prevent the opposite problem, overwatering, I test the soil moisture content with my finger before watering.

Watering container-grown herbs is critical for all gardeners, but it's of particular importance for those of us who live in arid climates. After years of parched-looking plants, I finally installed a drip system. What a difference! I use Antelco's emitters, called shrubblers (available from plumbing-supply stores and via mail order from The Urban Farmer Store, listed in the Resources section on page 104), as they are tailored so each container on the system can have the exact amount of water it needs. My drip system is connected to an automatic timer and scheduled to water every night for four minutes from spring through fall.

I enjoy planting Mexican herbs in colorful containers *(opposite)*. It's also an advantage when growing the tender varieties like culantro and *Lippia graveolens* as they are more readily brought inside when the weather gets cold. Here, in the blue pot, is Mexican tarragon; in the purple, an ornamental chili; next, a large pot of cilantro; and in the red pot, a Mexican basil. My patio a number of years ago was filled with herbs and chilis *(below)*. The chili plants included, from the left, a tall 'Chili d'Arbol,' a serrano, and a shorter chilipiquín all grown in a large wooden planter box. Another chilipiquín grows in a large blue pot.

the Anderson garden

That I grew a Mexican garden in California wouldn't be big news to most gardeners. But I knew most Mexican vegetables and herbs could be grown in northern gardens as well, and I needed a demonstration garden to prove it. Vermont sounded convincingly northern, so I approached Kit Anderson, my good friend and, at the time, managing editor of one of the country's finest gardening magazines, *National Gardening*, in Burlington, Vermont. Kit and I had worked on many projects together and I knew of her great interest in both Mexico and, of course, gardening.

We did some initial planning together, Kit did the ordering and the labor, and, after the harvest, I asked her to write a detailed account of her Vermont Mexican garden. It tickled me to invite one of the country's premier gardening writers to contribute an essay to this book. Kit loved the idea. Here's what she wrote:

"The eighteen-inch-tall statue of the Mexican corn god must have suspected something when I wrapped him in a blanket for the trip back from his native land to icy Vermont. Little did he know, but he had his work cut out for him. After all, our New England climate is not exactly suited for tropical crops. That's why we started planning the garden by crossing off those vegetables that wouldn't mature in a brief season. It meant we had to leave out chayote, jícama, and some of the southwestern flour corns and day-length-sensitive chiles. But we still had plenty to choose from: many chile peppers, tomatillos, bunching onions, cilantro, Mexican pinto beans and corn for drying, plus such necessities as tomatoes and squash.

"Growing heat-loving crops in Vermont isn't as absurd as it sounds. We grow fine peppers and tomatoes just about any year, and I've even had okra produce some summers. I live in a relatively warm part of the state, the Champlain Valley, which extends all along the western border and is almost at sea level. Our frost-free season often lasts close to 150 days, compared to the 90 to 120 usual in the mountains to the east. And it gets hot in midsummer.

"Nevertheless, we had to choose varieties carefully. After scanning a number of catalogs, we found a number of suitable varieties. Then came the design of the garden. I wanted it to have a Mexican feel to it, not be simply rows of crops that happened to be from that part of the world. Tropical gardens tend to be much less organized looking than the typical American garden. They're liable to consist of fruit trees, flowers, vegetables, and herbs, all growing in apparent disorder in the area around the house. Where sunshine is abundant, layered gardens make sense, with some crops growing in the shade of others, but without avocado trees and tamarind for shade, and with crops that would need all the sunshine they could get, our Vermont garden wasn't going to be layered—that approach just wouldn't work.

Kit Anderson's harvest from her Vemont Mexican garden.

"I compromised. The plan became a puzzle, with irregularly shaped beds each containing a combination of vegetables and flowers of different heights, and all planned so that sunshine would get everywhere. At the center, of course, would be the corn god.

"The next major challenge was the heavy clay soil in my garden. Even after adding a lot of organic matter, I can only harvest carrots after a heavy rain (and then I bring up huge globs of soil along with the roots.). Combine that with a cool, wet spring and you have about the worst possible conditions for heat-loving crops.

"Fortunately, we had a wonderful, early, relatively rain-free spring that year, so I was able to get in and till in April and incorporate much compost-ed manure. I still had a long wait before I could plant most of the crops. Our average last frost date here is May 15, but peppers hate to be cold. It does no good to set them out early; they'll only be stunted. In late April, I started cilantro, tomatillos, and 'Lemon Gem' marigolds in pots in my cold frame (a simple affair made of plastic).

"Encouraged by the warm weather, I set my pepper plants outside, let the young plants harden off (acclimatize outside) for a few days, and then put them out in the garden on about May 7, with individual wax-paper hot caps (little individual shelters) to protect them. The poor things needed all the help they could get because the weather turned cool and rainy for several weeks. Finally it warmed up again and I uncovered the peppers, as they were pushing up the hot caps. That night a ferocious storm blew in. My children watched in amazement as I screamed at the hail that was pounding the kitchen. But even that storm didn't faze those peppers. Except for a few ragged leaves, they looked just fine the next day.

"The little cilantro plants and the tomatillos went in next, along with a few cilantro seeds, a row of bunching onion seeds, and a few rows of pinto beans. By May 31, everything was planted, with the corn god occupying a place of honor in the center of the garden.

"To keep down weeds, I mulched with grass clippings around everything. The paths were cov-

ered first with newspapers, at least six-
teen pages thick, then with shredded
bark. Finally, I set up a combination
sprinkler and drip system. This last
step proved unnecessary, though, for
we headed into the coolest, wettest
summer I've ever experienced in
Vermont. Eggplants everywhere lan-
guished. Tomatoes ripened late.
Squash, even zucchini, produced poorly. We had great lettuce for tacos but
not much else to go with it. It seemed
impossible that the Mexican garden
would make it, but it plugged right
along. The peppers started bearing
fruit by late July and kept up through
September. The corn grew (slowly)
and matured beautiful ears. The
cilantro, especially the batch started
early, made a lot of greens before
going to seed. I cut it all back once,
froze the leaves, and then let the
plants go. The plants allowed to
mature produced seeds and from
these I got another harvest of leaves
later in the season. The beans were
fine until September; then I had to
take them into the barn to dry because
they started to sprout during a few late
rains. The tomatillos grew like mad,
overwhelming everything near them,
getting much larger than I'd planned.
The tomatillo is a low-growing, hulk-
ing sort of plant that needs its own
space. The amaranth I'd carefully
planned as a backdrop—with the sup-
posedly smaller yellow strain in front
and the red in back—did not cooper-
ate; the yellow turned out to be much
more vigorous, dwarfing the dramatic

red plants, which just peeked through from behind.

"The garden was at its best in late July, although the marigolds had been slow to begin flowering, so things weren't as colorful as I'd hoped they'd be. Tithonia, the Mexican sunflower, was a disappointment, too; it had lots of green foliage but flowered only late in the season.

"When corn harvest time came, my son and I had a wonderful time picking the ears and pulling off husks to reveal the richly colored kernels, everything from blue to red and yellow. I displayed some of the ears for months in a basket in our kitchen.

"Unfortunately, I never had time to develop great gourmet recipes with all these crops. We did feast on lots of tacos with chopped fresh tomatoes and cilantro and had salsas made of tomatillos, chiles, and green onions. I discovered I liked cilantro and have also used the frozen leaves for soups and in esquite, a corn dish sold on street corners that I had learned to love in Mexico."

Despite the problems, Kit's enthusiasm for her Mexican garden was constant and infectious. When I visited in July, the garden was beautiful and I was reassured to see everything doing so well. Even though I'd heard garden experts talk about growing chile peppers, cilantro, and tomatillos in northern climates, I found it much more convincing to see and touch the thriving plants myself.

19

encyclopedia of mexican vegetables

This encyclopedia covers, in detail, growing and preparing Mexican vegetables and herbs. Each vegetable is listed under its most common English name (which is often derived from its Spanish name), followed by the Spanish name, any alternate common names, and the Latin name. For major information on soil preparation, mulching, composting, and pests and diseases, see Appendices A and B in the back of the book. For further information on saving seeds, see page 4.

A number of seed companies carry Mexican or equivalent varieties of vegetables and herbs, as you will notice in the Resources section (page 102). As a side note: According to Craig

Dremann of the Redwood City Seed Company, to locate some of the old Mexican vegetable varieties we need to look overseas. Many vegetables that were taken from Mexico generations

ago show up in other countries still close to their ancient form. Two such examples are 'Ronde de Nice,' the round zucchinis common in France; and Costoluco-type fluted tomatoes from Italy. Therefore, you will find a number of varieties listed here that don't sound the slightest bit Mexican. For hard-to-find plants, I include source information under "Varieties." In addition, if you are searching for *any* edible plant, hard-to-find or otherwise, I highly recommend the ultimate source book, *Cornucopia II: A Source Book of Edible Plants,* by Steve Facciola.

Except for the watermelon, all the plants shown here—including grinding corns, summer and winter squash, and many types of peppers—have all evolved from plants native to Mexico and Central America. Though native to Africa, watermelons are very popular in Mexico.

AMARANTH

*Amaranthus hypochondriacus,
A. tricolor, A. cruentus,
A. gangeticus*

AMARANTH, A VALUABLE STAPLE of the Aztecs, was discouraged by the Spanish because it was associated with their sacrificial ceremonies. Nevertheless, these easily grown and nutritious plants are still enjoyed by modern-day Mexicans. Some types are grown for their leaves; other are grown for their edible and nutritious seeds, or grain. Leaf amaranths grow to about 18 inches. Grain amaranths are dramatic plants in the garden. With their large red or yellow plumes, they can reach 7 or 8 feet in height.

How to grow: Amaranth, a tropical annual, glories in warm weather. Start seedlings after all danger of frost is past. Plant seeds $^1/_8$ inch deep, 4 inches apart, in full sun and rich, well-drained soil. Plant the large grain amaranths in blocks with the rows 1 foot apart to prevent lodging (falling over); thin the plants to 1 foot apart. (If the plants start to lodge, place stakes and strings around the planting.) Plant the leaf types 6 inches apart and thin seedlings to 1 foot apart. Keep amaranths fairly moist. Generally, all amaranths grow with great enthusiasm. Cucumber beetles are occasionally a problem.

To harvest for greens, select the young, tender leaves and shoots. In the north, harvest the grains after the first frost; in mild-winter areas, wait until heads begin to drop their seed. Cut the

Burgundy grain amaranth 'Hopi Red Dye'

tops and lay them on a tarp to dry for about a week; protect against rain and heavy dew. To thresh large amounts of grain, lay the dry heads on a sheet or tarp, cover them with another sheet, and dance on the top layer to knock the shiny seeds free. For small amounts, you can rub the seed heads

on a screen or lightly beat them in a bag to remove the seed. Use an electric fan to separate the seeds from the lighter chaff as you pour them into a bowl. Wear gloves, as the flower heads can be rough and to prevent the red varieties from staining your hands.

Seed saving: Amaranths are primarily wind pollinated and readily cross-pollinate. To prevent cross-pollination, put cloth bags over the flower heads. Tape or tie the bags closed around the stalk. As the plants bear both male and female flowers, they self-pollinate with the bags in place. When the dried heads are ripe, cut them off and thresh as above.

Varieties

The leaves and seeds of all varieties can be eaten, but the leaf types have the tastiest leaves and the grain types more seeds. Native Seeds/SEARCH carries several varieties from Mexico; Abundant Life Seed Foundation and Bountiful Gardens carry many amaranths.

Grain Amaranths

'Alegria': grown in Mexico for its blond seed, which is used for the traditional confection called *alegria*

'Golden Giant': 110 days; 6 feet tall; golden flower heads; grown for its white grain and edible young leaves; high yielding

'Hopi Red Dye' ('Komo'): 120 days; to 6 feet tall; reddish purple leaves, black seeds

'K432' ('Plainsman'): 95 days; high-yielding variety from Rodale Research; light pink seed heads; good quality grain; carried by Johnny's Seeds and Southern Exposure Seed Exchange

'Mayo': 90 days; red-flowered, black-seeded variety from Sonora; grain used for pinole and atole and young leaves for quelites (greens); available from Bountiful Gardens

Leaf Amaranths

'Merah': 80 days; crinkled green and red leaves

How to prepare: Select young, tender leaves and shoots to use as you would spinach. Amaranth leaves are often served in a manner similar to other greens in Mexico (*quelites*)—namely, cook briefly in a large saucepan in the water used to wash them, or boil or steam them. Slice the cooked greens. Briefly sauté onions, chiles, and garlic in a little oil; add the amaranth and heat. Serve as a side dish or tuck in a tortilla with a little cheese. Add the mild-tasting leaves to soups and stews at the end of the cooking time.

The flavor of amaranth grain is quite mild and nutty, and it's high in protein. Amaranth flour contains no gluten, so it must be combined with wheat flour to make raised breads. The seed can be popped like popcorn; stir $1/2$ cup of seeds in a hot, dry frying pan until popped (about 30 seconds). Mix with honey to create alegria, a traditional confection from central Mexico. The seeds can be ground and added to moles and breads.

BEANS, SNAP, SHELLING, AND DRY
(FRIJOLES)
Phaseolus spp.

FAVA BEANS (HABAS, BROAD BEANS)
Vicia faba

RUNNER BEANS
P. coccineus

TEPARY BEANS
P. acutifolius

MOST OF THE WORLD'S BEANS are native to Mexico and are a staple food there. Fresh beans, particularly fava beans, during Lent, are served in a number of dishes, but cooked dry beans are the most common form.

Runner beans grow on large vines covered with spikes of scarlet red flowers. These flowers are followed by long string beans that are eaten fresh, or, later in the growing season, by the large shelled beans.

Tepary beans are an ancient bean type cultivated for centuries by the Papago Indians and other desert dwellers. Teparies are extremely heat, drought, and alkaline-soil tolerant. They are also very nutritious.

How to grow: The majority of cultivated beans are annuals that must be planted after all danger of frost is past.

Standard Snap, Shelling, and Dry Beans

Most beans have similar needs—namely, full sun and a good, loose garden loam with plenty of added humus. Sow seeds of bush beans 1 inch deep in rows 18 inches apart; thin to 6 inches. Pole beans need a strong trellis to climb on. Plant the seeds 1 inch deep; thin to 8 inches apart. If the plants look pale at midseason, fertilize with fish emulsion. Beans are best watered deeply and infrequently. They have their share of pests, including bean beetles, beanloopers, whiteflies, aphids, mites, and cucumber beetles. Anthracnose and leaf spots diseases are most prevalent in humid climates.

Harvest snap beans when the seeds inside are still very small and the pods are tender. For a continual crop, make sure to keep all beans harvested. Alternately, let the dry-bean varieties mature for a harvest of dry beans. See Harvesting Dry Beans, on page 25, for complete instructions.

Fava Beans

Fava beans are in another genus and grow in a different manner, as they prefer cool conditions and can tolerate light frosts. In cold-winter areas, plant fava beans when you plant peas. In areas where winters don't dip into the teens, plant favas in the fall. They need about 90 days of cool weather to produce well. To plant, prepare the soil and plant seeds 2 inches deep and about 3 inches apart. The plants grow quickly to 5 feet in height. Support the tall plants with stakes and strings surrounding the outsides of the beds.

Fava beans *(above);* and 'Windsor' fava beans *(right)*

Black aphids sometimes infest fava beans; control them with sprays of water or a commercial soap spray; slugs can destroy seedling beds.

For young, tender fava beans that do not need the skins removed, harvest when they first start to fill out the pods. Alternately, let the fava beans mature and use them for fresh shelling beans or let them dry in the pod for dry beans.

Runner Beans

Runner beans produce best in cool-summer areas. Grow them in good soil and in full sun. Plant the seeds in the ground 1 inch deep; thin to 6 inches apart. Keep the plants fairly moist and protect the seedlings from slugs, snails, and bean beetles. The plants flower within a few months and beans are produced if the weather stays cool or turns cool in early fall.

Harvest young runner bean pods for snap beans (the pods are larger than standard snap beans) or let the pods fill out and harvest for fresh shelling beans or for dried beans after the pods dry.

Tepary Beans

Tepary beans are fast-growing dry beans. Sow seeds in summer after the

Scarlet runner beans *(above)*; threshing dry beans in a bag *(below)*.

Harvesting Dry Beans: In rainy climates, drape plants over a crude drying frame or store them inside. In dry climates, let the pods dry completely in the garden and harvest the whole plant. Once the bean pods are completely dry, the seeds must be separated from the pods. For a small batch, shell the beans out by hand. For larger harvests, cut a 6-inch hole in the bottom corner of a burlap bag and tie it closed with a string. Put the plants in the bag and hang the bag on a branch or shed door; beat on it with a stick to loosen the beans from the pods. When most of the beans are free, hold a pan under the hole, untie the string, and empty the beans into the pan. Take out the chaff and repeat the process.

Clean the beans from the chaff. When the beans are completely dry, store them in a cool, dry place in containers that will keep bugs out. To prevent weevils, first put the containers in the freezer for 24 hours to kill the eggs.

Seed saving: Most beans are self-pollinating, so cross-pollination is usually not a problem. However, it is possible for insects to cause cross-pollination. To guard against crossing, separate varieties by 10 yards or put cages or cloth bags over the flowers. Runner beans are insect pollinated and therefore more likely to cross-pollinate. Harvest bean pods when they are dry, remove the seed, and continue to dry by laying the seed on a screen in a warm, dry room for a few weeks, stirring them every few days. When they are thoroughly dry, pack the seed in mason jars, label them, and freeze

soil has warmed. Plant in full sun, $\frac{1}{2}$ inch deep and 4 inches apart. Teparies are tolerant of heat and drought. Give them an initial deep watering at planting time (or plant just before a good summer rain) and then water after that only if the plants look stressed. Too much water causes the plants to produce foliage rather than pods. Teparies

have low resistance to bean mosaic virus, which may be transferred by seed; therefore, I recommend purchasing virus-free seed only.

Teparies are usually harvested for dry beans. Harvest the pods as they dry or harvest the whole plant once the pods are brown.

25

them for 24 hours to kill any weevils. Store in a cool, dry, dark place.

Varieties

Snap Beans

'Blue Lake': 62 days; pole; to 8 feet, productive; sweet, classic beany-flavored green pods; bush variety also available

'Kentucky Wonder' ('Old Homestead'): 68 days; pole; long, meaty pods popular since the mid-1800s and still great; plants are rust resistant; bush variety also available

Dry Beans

Hundreds of dry-bean varieties are grown in Mexico; here are but a few of the most popular.

'Black Mexican' ('Frijol Negro'): bush; small, black bean, most associated with southern Mexico

'Frijol Rojo' ('Red Mexican Chili'): semivining; popular in Mexico; grows to 4 feet; pods ripen after the plants drop leaves; resistant to bean beetles; most closely associated with central Mexico; available from Redwood City Seed Company

'Pinto': 90 days; can be grown as a pole bean; dry beans; most associated with northeastern Mexico and southwestern United States

'Peruano': a yellow, fairly small dry bean; bush bean popular in northwestern Mexico; available from Mexican grocery stores

Virus-Free White Tepary: small, white, virus-free tepary beans selected; available from Native Seeds/SEARCH

Beans, shown clockwise, from upper-left corner: pinto, giant pinto, scarlet runner, and Peruano

Virus-Free Yellow Tepary: ochre-colored, virus-free tepary beans; available from Native Seeds/SEARCH

Fava Beans

'Windsor': 80 days; bush; grows to 5 feet with green pods to 10 inches; large, light green beans

Runner Beans

'Aztec Scarlet Runner': 55 days; richly flavored pods; scarlet flowers; available from Plants of the Southwest

How to prepare: In Mexico, fresh snap beans are cooked with chiles, onions, garlic, and oil, or used in pork and egg dishes and in soups. Dry, however, is the favorite way Mexicans enjoy beans; dry beans are eaten nearly every day in a classic bean soup (see recipe for Frijoles de Olla on page 62) or in stews, tostadas, burritos (see recipe, page 84), and, of course, as creamy refried beans (see recipe, page 63). They can be stuffed into chiles or used as a filling for Mexican sandwiches (tortas). Runner beans are used in soups and in tamales.

Fava beans are used dry or fresh and are delicious combined with garlic, chiles, or both. Young fava beans have a special sweetness. Once these tasty beans are fully mature, they are shelled and then the bean skins must be peeled before preparation. Try them fresh or dried in a classic Mexican sauce with roasted tomatoes, onions, and garlic (see recipe, page 70).

Caution: Some males of Mediterranean descent are allergic to favas and should be wary when trying them for the first time. Persons taking antidepressants with monoamine inhibitors should avoid them at all costs.

'Fordhook Giant' chard

CHARD, SWISS
(ACELGA)
Beta vulgaris var. *flavescens*

CHARD IS A GREEN introduced into Mexico by the Spanish.

How to grow: Swiss chard tolerates a lot more heat than most greens, though it suffers in extreme heat, and is moderately hardy. Start it in early spring or late summer for mild-winter areas. Plant chard seeds $1/2$ inch deep, 6 inches apart, and thin to 1 foot. Plant in full sun and neutral soil with lots of added organic matter. For tender, succulent leaves, keep plants well watered. Mulch with a few inches of organic matter. When plants are about 6 weeks old, fertilize with $1/2$ cup balanced organic fertilizer for every 5 feet of row. A few pests and diseases bother chard, mainly slugs and snails (especially when the plants are young), and leaf miner, a fly larva.

To harvest chard, remove the outside leaves at the base; tender new leaves keep coming throughout the season.

Varieties
'Fordhook Giant': 60 days, a classic green chard with white ribs, fairly cold hardy

How to prepare: For centuries, the Mexican people harvested wild greens (*quelites*). Since their introduction by the Spanish, Swiss chard and, occasionally, spinach are often cooked in the same way as the quelites—namely, sautéed, steamed, or boiled until just done, and sliced or chopped. The greens are then added to seasoned sauces or vegetables—for example, a mixture of cooked onions, chiles, garlic, and other seasonings, like tomatoes and tomatillos. Alternately, the aromatic vegetables are puréed to make a sauce and the cooked greens—in this case, chard—added. This dish is served with tortillas. Chard can be added to green rice or to egg scrambles or combined with roasted poblanos and Mexican *crema* or new potatoes and tomatoes.

CHAYOTE

(CHAYOTE)

Sechium edule

CHAYOTES ARE NATIVE TO tropical America. This green, pear-shaped vegetable is versatile, absorbs seasonings well, and is much appreciated in Mexico. There, chayotes are creamy white or dark green and either thorny or smooth, while the chayotes we usually see in U.S. markets are medium green and smooth. As with summer squash, some varieties are delicately sweet and somewhat watery while others resemble potatoes in their starchiness.

How to grow: Chayotes are huge vines, 10 to 20 feet long, and are tender perennials that thrive only where winters are nearly frost free. Chayotes produce more fruit when more than one plant is present for cross-pollination.

To start your plants, buy three or so fruits at a produce market in late spring. (You only need one, but sometimes they rot.) I wait until the chayotes start to sprout on my kitchen windowsill and then plant them in one-gallon containers. I mostly cover the fruits with potting soil, leaving the shoot sticking out just above ground, and keep the soil moist but not wet. Shoots need lots of light, so I put them in a south-facing window or under grow lights. In a few weeks, the plants are established and I fertilize at this time with fish emulsion.

Once the weather is fully warmed up I plant the two chayotes a foot

apart, if I have limited room, 6 feet or more otherwise. Chayotes grow best in full sun in fertile, well-drained soil. Snails, slugs, and cucumber beetles are occasional problems. The vines, which need strong support, start to flower in the fall and to fruit 6 or 8 weeks later. (The spiny varieties take a longer season to flower and fruit.) Fruits are ready for harvesting when they are 3 or 4 inches in length. A vine can produce more than 50 fruits.

Starting chayote plants by planting the fruits *(above)* and the chayote fruit itself *(below)*.

How to prepare: The small fruits can be eaten without peeling, but the skin must be removed on mature ones. Be aware, though: when you peel raw chayotes, they exude a sticky substance. It can be removed by washing and rubbing, but some cooks wear rubber gloves or parboil the fruit for a few minutes before peeling. The smooth, light green chayotes have a mild, less pronounced flavor than the spiny or dark green ones. According to Juvenal Chavez, owner of Mi Pueblo stores in San José, the spiny chayotes are considered more flavorful and preferred for simple dishes that showcase the fruit.

In Mexican cuisine, chayotes are most often steamed or boiled for about 15 minutes, seasoned with butter, salt, and pepper, and served with salsa, or combined with garlic, chiles, and, sometimes, tomatoes (see recipe, page 00), and sautéed. Recipes occasionally call for adding chayote slices to soups or steaming and cutting them in thick slices, making a sandwich of them with cheese in between, and dipping them in egg batter and cooking them like chiles rellenos. A salad of steamed and cooled chayote can be dressed with lime juice or vinegar and mixed with tomatoes and onions. The men I met at the Mi Tierra community gardens in San José enjoy them steamed and mashed with milk and honey or baked in aluminum foil in the oven like baked potatoes. Chayotes are sometimes made into a dessert by stuffing them with a mixture of eggs, sugar, spongecake crumbs, and seasonings and baking them.

CHIA
(CHÍA)
Salvia hispanica

MEXICAN CHIA IS MOST FAMILIAR to Americans as those cute little Chia Pets in the TV commercials. A number of plants are called chia; another one, *S. columbariae,* referred to as desert or golden chia, is native to California and the Baja peninsula. The seeds of both can be used to make a refreshing summer drink.

How to grow: Plant the seeds of chia in spring in very fast-draining soil in full sun. They grow 2 to 3 feet tall and produce small blue flowers. Good drainage is essential, as most sages die readily in heavy clay or soggy soil.

Harvest the dried seed stalks and, when completely dry, winnow off the seed pods and chaff from the seeds.

Varieties

The easiest way to obtain chia seeds is to purchase a package at a Mexican market, where it is usually offered on racks with other Mexican herbs. Seeds of chias are also carried by J. L. Hudson, Plants of the Southwest, and Native Seeds/SEARCH.

How to prepare: Chia is primarily used to make a cooling drink called *agua con chía*. Place a tablespoon of chia seeds in a pitcher and add a quart of water. Let sit for an hour or so until the seeds have become gelatinous and swell. When ready to serve, add limes and sugar to taste, stir, and pour the seeds and juice over ice. Less traditionally, chia leaves can be used to flavor poultry and meats, and the sprouted seeds can be sprinkled on salads to give a peppery taste.

Chia

Cilantro in flower *(left)* and cilantro *(above)*

CILANTRO ET AL.

(cilantro, fresh coriander,
Chinese parsley)

Coriandrum sativum

CULANTRO

(cilantro, cilantrillo, Mexican
coriander)

Eryngium foetidum

PAPALOQUELITE

(papalo)

Porophyllum ruderale ssp.
macrocephalum

CILANTRO (BETTER KNOWN AS
coriander throughout much of the
world) is native to the Mediterranean
and has been cultivated for over 3,000

years, beginning with the ancient
Egyptians. Culantro and papaloquelite, on the other hand, are native
to Mexico and South America. What
all three of these herbs have in common is a similar flavor and aroma people either love or hate. I, for one, crave
the earthy flavor.

Cilantro, which looks something
like parsley, is widely used in Mexican
cuisine—both the fresh leaves, called
cilantro, and the ripe seeds, called
coriander. Culantro is a tender perennial herb with long, incised leaves that
takes hotter weather than cilantro and,
unlike cilantro and papaloquelite, can
also be successfully dried, retaining its
characteristic flavor and color.
According to herb maven Carole
Saville, papaloquelite tastes similar to
cilantro but has a more complex flavor,
which she describes as "sort of like
gazpacho in a leaf, sans tomatoes."

How to grow: Contrary to what lots
of gardeners think, the annual cilantro
is easy to grow; you just need to know
its idiosyncrasies. Cilantro needs cool
weather and bolts to seed readily when
days start to lengthen in the spring and
when weather becomes warm.
Therefore, it is best planted in the fall.

In cold-winter areas, it can be planted
as a quick fall crop before a heavy frost
hits, or the seeds can be planted in late
fall to sprout the next spring after the
ground thaws. In mild-winter areas,
fall-planted cilantro grows lush and
tall over winter. (Cilantro tolerates
light frosts.) In short-spring areas,
early plantings are more successful
than late. One guaranteed way to grow
under these conditions is to treat it as a
cut-and-come-again crop. Plant seeds 1
inch apart and snip 3-inch-tall
seedlings above ground level; replant
every 2 weeks until the weather gets too
warm.

When possible, start cilantro from
seeds in place, as it resents transplanting
(another reason cilantro bolts readily).
Plant seeds $1/4$ inch deep in rich, light
soil and in full sun. Thin the
seedlings to 6 inches and keep moist.
The varieties most commonly available in nurseries, while adequate, are
bred to quickly bolt and produce
seeds (coriander) for the world seed
trade. If you choose varieties bred for
leaf production instead, available
from mail-order seed companies,
you'll harvest leaves for a longer time.
Fertilize if plants get pale. Except for
slugs, cilantro has few pests and diseases. Harvest cilantro sprigs once
plants are 6 inches tall.

Culantro is treated as a short-lived
perennial in warm-climate zones.
Below Zone 9, it is grown as an annual.
Sow seeds indoors in early winter and
set seedlings out when the soil has
warmed. (Seeds are slow to germinate.)
Grow culantro in moderately fertile,
fast-draining, moist soil in full sun. In

warm climates, grow it in filtered sun. It may also be grown in containers and wintered over inside. Culantro grows to 2 feet tall, with a rosette of sharply toothed, oblong basal leaves (ones growing from the crown at the base of the plant) about 4 inches long and 1 inch wide. Flowering stems grow to about 18 inches. Keep flowering stems cut back for a continual harvest of the basal leaves. Control slugs and snails.

One plant of papaloquelite is usually sufficient. It is a warm-weather annual that is easily grown if the seed is sown after the weather is reliably warmed. (It can also be started indoors 6 weeks before the last frost date.) It does best in full sun and in a well-drained, sandy soil. Give regular water. The plant can reach 6 feet but stays smaller in most areas. The leaves are best harvested when the plant is young.

Varieties

Choose cilantro varieties designated as slow-bolting, available from Shepherds, Nichols, and Johnny's. Papaloquelite and culantro are carried by Richters.

How to prepare: Cilantro leaves are used fresh, as the flavor fades quickly when cooked. Generally, they are chopped and sprinkled on a dish or mixed in after cooking to give a characteristic flavor. Add the chopped leaves sparingly to tacos, guacamole, and bean and corn dishes, fold it into cooked vegetable dishes, salsas, moles, ceviche and other fish dishes, or use whole leaves as a garnish. The essential oils in cilantro fade quickly and there

Culantro (*above*) and papaloquelite (*below*)

is no successful way to preserve its flavor.

In Mexico, the aromatic leaves of culantro are classically used in soups and stocks, added at the end of cooking. Culantro is a versatile herb that can be used in any dish where you want the taste of cilantro. It's great with ground cumin when added to guacamole. In some regions of Mexico, the flower heads of culantro are used as a spice to flavor moles. Sprinkle a chicken or bean taco with *queso fresca* and chopped culantro leaves to appreciate its characteristic flavor.

In her book, *Exotic Herbs,* Carole Saville says that some restaurants in Mexico keep sprigs of culantro in a glass of water on the table so diners can pluck leaves "to add to bean dishes or roll up in a warm tortilla." She recommends it in tomato salsa, especially chipotle salsa, and in any dish where you would use cilantro. Craig

Dremann of the Redwood City Seed Company says some people choose food stands in Mexico by whether they serve cilantro or papaloquelite. Those serving papaloquelite offer more authentic dishes.

Mexican corn

CORN
(MAIZ: DRY CORN; ELOTE: FRESH CORN OR CORN ON THE COB)
Zea mays

DENT CORN
Z. m. var. *indentata*

SWEET CORN
Z. m. var. *saccharata*

CORN WAS DOMESTICATED in Mexico about 2000 B.C. and it is the foundation of Mexican cooking. Most Mexican varieties are intended to be used dried. Dent, often called field corn, not sweet corns, predominate in Mexico, and there are numerous local varieties. Some are used for making tortillas; others have large, plump kernels best for *pozole,* a hominy-based soup. Yet others are a bit sweeter; picked when the kernels are mature but still juicy, they are roasted or used for fresh corn tamales or soups. The super-sweet types of corn preferred north of the border are not popular in Mexico.

If you enjoy Mexican cooking, a real advantage of growing your own corn is that you will have lots of husks and corn leaves in which to wrap your tamales.

How to grow: Corn requires both summer heat and full sun and is generally planted from seeds sown directly into the garden. Corn pollen is transferred by the wind from the male flower (the tassel) onto the pistil of the female flower (the silk). If corn is planted in long single rows, the silks won't be well pollinated. Instead, plant a block of shorter multiple rows, a minimum of four being needed. Plant seeds in rich soil, 1 inch deep, 4 inches apart, with 3 feet between rows. Thin corn seedlings to 1 foot apart.

Before planting your dent corns, work a source of organic nitrogen (such as aged chicken manure or blood meal) into the soil. Once the seedlings are established, lightly side dress with fish emulsion. If the leaves begin to pale or the plants aren't growing vigorously, apply more fish emulsion. (The sweet corns most commonly grown in American home gardens, including the 'Golden Bantam' [listed on page 33], are heavier feeders and require higher levels of nitrogen throughout the growing season.) Side dress the dent corns at tasseling time with about half of what you'd fertilize American sweet corns. Most dent corns are drought tolerant. With all corn, however, attention to water at tasseling time helps guard against poorly filled out ears. The dent corns generally grow to 10 to 14 feet, taller than most sweet corns.

The corn earworm is the most common insect pest. They can be smothered by a bit of mineral oil squirted into the ear just as the silk is beginning to dry, or apply *Bacillus thuringiensis* to the plant. Other insect pests include corn borers, southern corn rootworms, corn flea beetles, and seed corn maggots. Birds can steal the seeds out of the ground, so cover new plantings. The most common corn diseases are Stewart's bacterial wilt, southern corn leaf blight, and corn smut. The latter, a fungus, is considered a delicacy in Mexico—think wild mushrooms. Called *huitlachoche,* the fungus is harvested when plump and gray, before it gets black and dry.

Sweet corn is ready to eat when the silks are dry and brown and the ears are well filled out. Test for ripeness by puncturing a few kernels with a fingernail. Unripe kernels squirt a watery liquid, ripe ones a milky juice. Most varieties of sweet corn begin to lose their sweetness as soon as they are picked, so it is best to harvest ears as close to cooking time as possible.

Harvest dent corns for grilling and fresh corn tamales after the silks turn brown and the kernels are milky and still sweet. For dry dent corn, leave the ears on the plant until the kernels are dry. If the weather is very wet, cut the stalks after the husks begin to turn brown and store them in a dry place. When the corn is completely dry—which can take weeks—husk the ears and store them in a dry place, or remove the kernels and store them in sealed jars.

Seed saving: Corn is wind pollinated and cross-pollinates easily. At least 300 feet must separate different varieties tasseling at the same time; 1,000 feet is better. Varieties with tassel times 2 weeks apart may be planted somewhat closer. Hand pollinate to ensure full ears, using pollen from one plant to pollinate another plant—never the same plant. Select the earliest and fullest ears, mark them with a piece of ribbon, and allow them to dry in place until they are ripe for seed harvest. Peel back the husks, hang the ears in an airy place, and allow the kernels to continue to dry on the cob until they can be twisted loose with relative ease. Store in an airtight container. For long-term storage, store whole ears.

Varieties

For the largest selection of Mexican varieties, contact Native Seeds/SEARCH. If you live in southern latitudes, you might want to buy corn kernels (usually pozole types) from a Mexican market these are primarily dent varieties—and grow them out. (These varieties take a very long season to produce—160 days—and seldom produce in northern latitudes.) For more assured production, try some of the following earlier varieties.

'Aztec Red': 160 days; huge red kernels; dent type; 10-foot plants with large ears; adapted to Southwest; use for hominy or pozole, same as red ones in U.S. Mexican markets; carried by Redwood City Seed Company

'Golden Bantam 8 Row': 75 days; yellow sweet corn; heirloom; 6-inch ears on 5-foot stalks; classic corn taste

'Hickory King': 85 days fresh, 115 days dry; white dent; large kernels; good for roasting ears while young; excellent for hominy; robust plants, adaptable; resistant to beetles and earworms; tolerates blights; available from Bountiful Gardens and Southern Exposure Seed Exchange

'Northstine Dent': 100 days; yellow grinding corn; 8-inch ears on 7-foot stalks; early, good for short-season areas

'Pozole': 100 days; large white kernels for hominy; 12 feet tall; drought tolerant; available from Plants of the Southwest

'Reid's Yellow Dent': 110 days; heirloom; use for roasting ears; 9-inch ears on 7-foot stalks; adapted to southern conditions

How to prepare: In Mexican cuisine, corn appears at almost every meal. The most common form is a dent corn that has been hominied and made into tortillas. The hominy process involves treating dent corn with powdered slaked lime to help remove the skins, which also helps to even out the available protein. Corn treated with lime is called *nixtamal* and can be used whole as hominy in soups and stews called *pozole* but, more commonly, the treated

The gray, swollen kernels of the corn fungus, huitlachoche

corn is ground to produce *masa*. *Nixtamal* is easily made from garden corn with no special equipment and is well worth the effort to make your own pozole. In contrast, making *masa* for tortillas and tamales requires a grain mill able to grind the corn into a smooth paste that is then formed into flat, round, corn tortillas or thick boat-shaped *sopes,* or used as the filling for corn-husk-wrapped tamales—the mainstay of Mexican meals since ancient days. Rick and Deann Bayless, in *Authentic Mexican,* give detailed instructions on how to make your own tortillas and tamales from scratch. To hominy your corn for pozole, see page 65.

Fresh dent and, less frequently, sweet corn is grilled in Mexico. It can be dipped in cream and sprinkled with chili powder (see recipe, page 63) and eaten off the cob; kernels can be cut off the cob and added to soups, stews, and relishes.

The most common recipe for *huitlachoche,* the corn fungus, is to cook it briefly with chiles and onions and use it for a filling in quesadillas.

Cumin

CUMIN
(COMINO)
Cuminum cyminum

CUMIN IS ANOTHER Mediterranean herb now used to flavor many dishes in Mexico. It can be grown only by those who live in long, hot growing seasons.

How to grow: Under the right conditions, cumin grows to about 1 foot tall with slender branching stems, long, narrow leaves, and clusters of white flowers. It is fussy about climate and many folks, including myself, have had it grow for a while and then just decline, never producing its tasty seeds. Whether it doesn't get enough heat or is sensitive to day length is yet to be determined.

If you want to try it, seeds can be sown indoors in early winter and transplanted outdoors when the weather has warmed. According to the literature, it generally takes up to 4 months for cumin seeds to mature. Thresh the seeds, dry them, and store in airtight jars. For best flavor, toast and grind the dried seeds just before using. And good luck.

Varieties

Generic cumin is carried by Richters.

How to prepare: Whole cumin seeds can be used in marinades for pork, chicken, and fish. A pinch of the ground seed gives guacamole charac-

ter, and cumin's robust character stands up to the spicy ingredients in chili, cheese enchiladas, and tamales. It is also tasty in *mole verde,* a sauce made with green tomatillos that is spooned over poached chicken breasts, and is a must in my refried beans.

Epazote

EPAZOTE
(EPAZOTE, PAZOTE)
Chenopodium ambrosioides

EPAZOTE IS A PUNGENT HERB shaped like a goosefoot, one of its common names. It is widely used in cooking in central and southern Mexico and the Yucatán. Like cilantro, epazote has its detractors, for its leaves have an aggressive, resinous scent. But for aficionados, the herb is addictive and is indispensable in a bowl of black beans.

How to grow: Epazote is so easily grown that it actually grows wild in many temperate areas of the United States, even in urban vacant lots. If you don't pick the seed heads off, the plant can become a weed in your garden. It is easily started from seed in spring, will grow to a height of 3 to 4 feet, and needs some pruning to look tidy.

Harvest leaves and shoots and use as seasoning. Freeze or dry the leaves, or bring a containerized plant inside for winter use.

Varieties

Epazote is carried by Plants of Southwest, Richters, and Native Seeds/SEARCH.

How to prepare: Epazote has been used in Mexico for centuries, particularly with black beans, and can be used to season soups, corn, squash, mushrooms, fish, and seafood dishes. Mexicans use epazote to help control flatulence from eating beans. The herb also flavors pork and chicken tamales and cheese quesadillas. Its assertive quality makes it a good addition to a mole or a fiery tomato salsa. Epazote retains its flavor when dried. While epazote is a popular culinary herb, it should be used in moderation. Also, it is sometimes difficult to find epazote in markets so it can often be substituted with a combination of cilantro and lemon grass in many recipes.

HOJA SANTA
(HIERBA SANTA, HOJA DE ACUYO)
Piper auritum

HOJA SANTA IS AN AROMATIC herb with large heart-shaped, anise-scented leaves, and it is referred to in a number of Mexican cookbooks. It is used in southern Mexico as a wrapping for tamales and fish and is chopped to flavor soups, sauces, and eggs. Several specialty herb nurseries carry the herb. However, hoja santa's volatile oils contain safrole, which is also found in sassafras. In 1960, the Food and Drug Administration banned sassafras bark, sassafras oil, and safrole as flavoring agents because of their carcinogenic properties, so the safety of flavoring food with hoja santa is questionable.

Hoja Santa

35

HUAUZONTLÍ
(GUAUZONCLES)

Chenopodium berlanderi
(C. nuttaliae)

HUAUZONTLÍ IS GROWN IN Mexico for its edible leaves, which are eaten like spinach, and its bushy unripe seed heads, which are an unusual treat.

How to grow: Huauzontlí is an annual plant that is started indoors from seed and transplanted into the garden when the nights are above 50°F. Plant in full sun and good soil. The plants tolerate heat well. Keep fairly moist during the growing season. In autumn, the leaves turn reddish brown.

Varieties

Generic huauzontlí is carried by Richters and Native Seeds/SEARCH.
'Aztec Red Spinach': 60 days; grows to 2 feet high and 1 foot across; leaves are magenta when starts to flower; cooks in less than a minute in boiling water; retains color after cooking; carried by Redwood City Seed Company

How to prepare: The mild-tasting shoots and young leaves can be prepared as you would spinach. In Mexico, huauzontlí is interchangeable in dishes using the leaf amaranth described on page 23. A traditional way of cooking seed heads of huauzontlí, as described in Diana Kennedy's book *The Cuisines of Mexico,* is to harvest the top 4 to 5 inches of the branches when they are covered with green seed heads and blanch them; then put small bunches together with cheese, dip in egg batter, and fry. The dried seeds can be combined with different wheat and corn flours for flavor.

Huauzontlí

Jamaica plant

Jamaica calyx ready for harvest

JAMAICA
(FLORES DE JAMAICA, HIBISCUS, ROSELLE)
Hibiscus sabdariffa

THIS HERB IS AN EDIBLE hibiscus grown for its dried flowers, which are used to make a tart red beverage also called jamaica. The "flower" is actually the calyx, which is the outer covering of the flower.

How to grow: Jamaica grows to about 5 feet tall with large, flat-lobed greenish red or red leaves and small yellow flowers. Jamaica needs a long growing season. (USDA Zones 8–11) to produce enough calyxes for collection. Sow the seeds indoors in early winter for transplanting when the weather is warm, or sow directly into the ground in early spring. Jamaica is best grown in average soil with full sun and moderate water. Feed once a month with fish emulsion during the growing season.

Varieties

It's About Thyme carries generic jamaica.

How to prepare: If you have had Red Zinger tea, you have enjoyed the flavor of jamaica, which is one of its primary ingredients and gives the tea its red color. The traditional jamaica beverage is made with an infusion of the dried flower calyxes sweetened with sugar (see recipe, page 89). It can be served hot or cold and is sometimes mixed with fruit juices, especially orange juice.

JÍCAMA
(JÍCAMA)
Pachyrhizus tuberosus

JÍCAMA, A NATIVE OF TROPICAL
America, is a crispy, sweet root vegetable commonly eaten raw.

How to grow: Jícama is a tender
perennial vine that can reach 20 feet in
length and is grown as an annual in
the United States. It is planted from
seeds and takes 8 to 9 months to produce large tubers, but if started inside
early, in a frost-free growing season of
about 5 months, it produces small but
high-quality tubers. Plant in full sun in
fairly moist and well-fertilized soil.
Harvest the tubers when the plants die
back in the fall.

Caution: Do not eat the seeds or
pods, as they are poisonous.

Varieties
Generic jícama is carried by Redwood
City Seed Company, J. L. Hudson,
Chiltern Seeds, and Horticultural
Enterprises.

How to prepare: This juicy, sweet
vegetable is eaten either raw or lightly
cooked. To prepare, peel off the brown
skin and slice or dice. In Mexico, sticks
of jícama are often dipped raw in chili
powder and/or lime juice and eaten as
a crudité, eaten in a salad with cilantro
(see recipe, page 75), or combined with
melons, tropical fruits, and citrus and
dusted with chili powder (see recipe,
page 73).

Jícama fruit *(above)*; jícama in flower *(below)*

'Iceberg' lettuce

LETTUCE
(LECHUGA)

Lactuca sativa

THE SPANIARDS INTRODUCED lettuce to Mexico long ago and it remains a popular salad green.

How to grow: Lettuce is a cool-season annual crop that can be grown in most areas of the country. Most varieties go to seed or become bitter rapidly once hot weather arrives. In warm weather, lettuce grows better with afternoon or filtered shade. In mild-winter areas, lettuce grows through the winter.

Lettuce prefers a soil high in organic matter. It needs regular moisture and profits from light feedings of fish emulsion every few weeks. Sow seeds 1/8 inch deep outdoors, start seeds indoors in flats, or buy transplants. You can start lettuce outside as soon as you can work the soil in spring. Plant seeds 2 inches apart and 1/8 inch deep. Keep seed beds uniformly moist until seedlings appear. Thin seedlings to 6 to 12 inches apart, depending on the variety. Failure to thin seedlings can result in disease problems.

Protect seedlings from birds, slugs, snails, and aphids until they grow fairly large. Botrytis, a gray mold fungus disease, can cause the plants to rot off at the base. Downy mildew, another fungus, causes older leaves to get whitish patches and eventually die.

You can harvest lettuce at any stage. If possible, harvest during the cool of the day. Heading lettuces are generally harvested by cutting off the head at the soil line.

Varieties

'Cos Paris White': 80 days; heirloom; large romaine type with medium green leaves; good for fall and mild winters

'Iceberg': 70 days; heirloom for the home garden; tight heads; mosaic resistant; available from Fox Hollow Seeds

How to prepare: Due to overexposure and abuse, 'Iceberg' lettuce has fallen out of favor, but a well-grown, crispy sweet head is perfect with many Mexican dishes. In Mexico, whole leaves of lettuce are occasionally used to line a salad plate or to scoop up appetizers. The most common presentations, though, are sliced thinly to serve as a garnish for pozole, stews, and soups, and in tacos, tostadas, and burritos.

MARIGOLD, MEXICAN
(ANISILLO, PERICON, MEXICAN TARRAGON)
Tagetes lucida

THIS TRADITIONAL PUNGENT herb is used for an infusion (tisane) with a strong anise overtone. The plant is also used to decorate the house on the Mexican equivalent of Halloween.

How to grow: Mexican marigold is an easily grown, tender perennial that reaches 3 feet in height and is grown as an annual in cold climates. Its foliage sprawls if not cut back a few times a year. In cold climates, the plant is covered with small marigold-type flowers in the fall; in mild-winter areas, it can bloom all winter. Sow seeds in early spring indoors and transplant outside in a sunny spot after the weather warms up. Every spring, cut the plant back to the ground and fertilize; it will quickly sprout from the crown.

Varieties

Generic Mexican marigold/tarragon is carried by Native Seeds/SEARCH, Redwood City Seeds, J. L. Hudson, Richters, and Well-Sweep Herb Farm.

How to prepare: Mexican marigold leaves are used primarily for an infusion or herbal tea that makes an unusual anise-scented accompaniment to *pan dulce* and other pastries. It has a special affinity for corn, squash, and poultry—turkey, in particular. It can be substituted for French tarragon, although lesser amounts should be used because of its pronounced anise flavor. Mexican tarragon dries well for winter use.

Mexican tarragon

40

MELONS

CANTALOUPE (MELON)

Cucumis melo var. *reticulatus*

WATERMELON (SANDIA)

Citrullus lanatus

MELONS ORIGINATED IN THE heat of West Africa, were refined in Central Asia, and brought to the New World by immigrants.

How to grow: Melons are warm-season annuals that need heat to produce superior sweet fruit. After all chance of frost is past, sow seeds where they are to grow. In short-summer areas, start seeds indoors and move seedlings into the garden after the soil is warm and the weather settled. Melons are usually grown in hills spaced 6 to 8 feet apart, with two or three plants 6 inches apart in a hill. They can also be planted in rows 6 to 8 feet apart with 2 feet between plants.

Melons need full-sun locations, rich, well-drained soil, and ample water during the growing season. Prepare the soil by adding much organic matter, including a few shovelfuls of chicken manure and a half cup bone meal for each hill. Side dress with fish emulsion when fruits are starting to set. Keep young plants well weeded. In cool climates, a black plastic mulch around these heat-loving plants raises the soil temperature. (See more about this in Appendix A.) Reduce watering toward harvest time. Too much water then results in insipid fruits and uneven watering can actually split the melons.

Young melon plants are susceptible to cutworms and snails. Squash vine borers and striped or spotted cucumber beetles can be problems.

Downy and powdery mildew is sometimes a problem, particularly late in the season. Choose mildew-resistant varieties if this is a problem in your area. Rotate your crops to help prevent diseases.

Allow fruits to remain on the vine until they are fully ripe, as a melon's full sugar content is not reached until the last few days of growth. Cantaloupe is ready to harvest when its netting has turned from green to tan, it smells rich and fragrant, and it easily detaches from the stem. Watermelon is ripe when the fruit's surface skin is dull and difficult to puncture with your fingernail, when the bottom of the melon has passed through green to yellow, and when the tendrils on the stem near the fruit are brown.

'Ambrosia' melon

Varieties

'Ambrosia': 86 days; luscious, extra-sweet cantaloupe with thick flesh; resistant to powdery mildew; available from Burpee

'Hale's Best': 88 days; 3-pound cantaloupes, sweet flavor; resistant to drought and powdery mildew

'Sugar Baby': 85 days; probably best watermelon for the family garden; small fruits; dark green rind

'Georgia Rattlesnake': 90 days; Southern favorite watermelon with firm, sweet, rose pink flesh; light green skin with dark strips; 35 pounds; carried by Seed Savers Exchange and R. H. Shumway's

How to prepare: Melons are popular in Mexico and are also often combined with tropical fruits, especially in a salad dusted with chili powder (see recipe, page 73). Melon fruit is also used in a cooling drink, sometimes with limes or tequila (see recipe, page 88). Cantaloupe seeds are sometimes ground and used for a cooling drink as well.

MINTS
SPEARMINT (YERBA BUENA)
Mentha spicata

PEPPERMINT (MENTHA)
M. x piperita

IN MEXICO, *YERBA BUENA*, meaning "good herb," usually denotes spearmint, though a few other *Mentha* (mint) species and a savory, *Satureja douglasii,* which has a similar fragrance, are frequently enjoyed.

How to grow: Mints are perennial plants; most are hardy to USDA Zone 5, grow to about 2 feet, and can be quite rangy. If not contained, most mints can become pests. Because they spread via underground runners, they are best planted in containers or within rings of metal flashing in the ground. Most mints prefer moist, sun to part-sun conditions. Set out plants in the spring. Prune heavily twice a year to keep plants under control. Under some conditions, mints are prone to whitefly infestations. Rust is another occasional problem. If you have a serious infestation of either, start new plants where you have better air circulation. Once mint plants are growing vigorously, they can be harvested anytime throughout the year.

Varieties
Generic spearmint and peppermint are readily available at local nurseries as well as through mail-order nurseries. *Satureja douglasii* is carried by Well-Sweep Herb Farm and Goodwin Creek Gardens.

How to prepare: All the mints have a characteristic clean minty flavor. The leaves are best used fresh, but they can be preserved by freezing and drying.

In Mexico, spearmint is used in some moles and in green pozole. Its chopped leaves are particularly tasty in albondigas, little meatballs, generally served in a tomato sauce; it also gives a nice fragrance to soups, especially chicken and tomato. Both mints are also used in cool drinks and in salads.

ONIONS
BULBING ONIONS (CEBOLLAS)
Allium cepa

GARLIC (AJO)
A. sativum

BOTH WHITE ONIONS AND scallions are used in Mexican cooking. Yellow onions are seldom compatible with Mexican foods, as they are either too mild or too sweet.

How to grow: The onion family prefers cool weather, particularly in the juvenile stages, and grows best in well-drained soil rich in organic matter and phosphorus. They are heavy feeders and should be fertilized, as well as evenly watered, throughout the growing season.

Bulbing Onions
Bulbing onions are grown from seeds or from young bulbs, called sets. As biennials, onions bulb the first year when grown from seed and flower the second if they are replanted. When planted from sets, they usually both bulb and flower the first year.

It is important to select the right variety of onion for your climate and time of year because the bulbs are formed according to day length. Short-day onions bulb when they get 10 to 12 hours of light per day and are most successful when fall-planted in southern latitudes. Long-day onions require about 16 hours of sunlight each day to bulb; they are ideal for northern areas. Medium-day onions require 12 to 14

Large and small Mexican-style onions *(above)*, and garlic plants *(below)*

The most common pests attacking onions are thrips and the fly larva known as the onion maggot. Thrips are attracted to stressed onion plants, especially those that are moisture stressed.

Onions may be harvested from scallion stage to mature bulbs. Storage onions are harvested after their tops die down—a process you can hasten by bending the tops over. To harvest, dig up the onions and let them stay on top of the soil to dry out for at least a day. Protect from sunburn by covering them with their tops. Place them on a screen where air circulation is good to allow the skins to dry for several weeks before their final storage.

Varieties

The intensity of onions can vary considerably on where in the country it is grown and in what type of soil it is planted.

'Early Supreme': 160 days, fall planted; white, short-day onion with mild flesh; available from Lockhart Seeds

'Evergreen Hardy White': 60 days; hardy perennial; white bunching onion; highly resistant to freezing; may be left in the ground year-round; resists thrips, smut, and pink root; needs only occasional division of clumps once established

'Southport White Globe' ('White Globe'): 110 days; long-day, medium-sized onion with white skin and flesh; pungent; adaptable

'White Lisbon': 60 days; an *Allium cepa* developed for use as a scallion; tender green tops and long white stems; does well in a variety of soils

hours of light each day and do well in most parts of the country.

Start seeds inside in late winter or sow onion seeds outside 1/4 inch deep, 2 inches apart in spring or, in mild climates, in fall; alternately, put out sets planted 4 inches apart. While many gardeners plant onions in rows or wide beds, they can be interplanted with other vegetables. Fertilize with a balanced organic fertilizer when plants are about 6 inches tall and beginning to bulb. Depending on the variety, onions should be thinned to give ample room for the bulbs. Use the thinnings as "knob onion" or scallions, depending on their size. Water the plants regularly while they are growing; once the bulbs stop enlarging, discontinue watering while they finish maturing.

Braided garlic

Garlic

Garlic plants are grown from cloves that are purchased in heads from nurseries. Plant in the fall or early spring. Ample and consistent water is needed for the first 4 or 5 months of development, as is full sun.

Divide the heads into individual cloves and plant them about 1 inch deep and 4 inches apart. Garlic does best in soil with much added organic matter. In areas of extremely cold winters, mulch with straw to protect fall-started plants. Garlic is hardy to all but the most severe cold and is virtually free of pests and diseases. Garlic greens may be lightly harvested and used in cooking as you would scallions. Garlic is ready for harvest when the plant tops turn brown and die back. Dig the heads carefully and allow them to dry on a screen in the shade. Store them in a cool, dry area with good air circulation.

Varieties

Filaree Farms specializes in organically grown garlic, and Territorial Seed Company carries many varieties.

'Gilroy California Late': good flavor; long keeping

'German Extra-Hardy': winter-hardy; good for northern gardens; keeps well

'Spanish Roja': midseason; popular hardneck type with true garlic flavor; sometimes called Greek garlic

How to prepare: White onions are one of the main seasonings in Mexican cuisine, though the red ones are occasionally used, especially for pickling and to garnish a dish. When used, raw onions are generally treated to tame the bite by either running the chopped or sliced pieces under running water for a few minutes, pouring boiling water over them, or marinating them for a half hour or so in lime juice or vinegar. They are then drained and often used as a garnish to sprinkle over pozole, stews, soups, tostadas, and salsas. They are a popular addition to burritos, tacos, tortas, and salads. Toasting onions on a comal, discussed on page 68, is often the first step in making cooked sauces, moles, and meat stews. Small, fresh white onions, about an inch or more in diameter, with their leaves attached, are popular grilled (see recipe, page 68) and served sliced in a soft, warm taco with grilled meats. Onions pickled in vinegar or lime juice with oregano or other seasonings are ubiquitous additions to the Mexican table. Whole, small white onions and sliced large white or red ones are sometimes pickled by themselves but, more often, they are combined with chiles and garlic.

OREGANOS, MEXICAN
(OREGANO)
Lippia graveolens, Poliomentha longiflora

RECENTLY, HERB RESEARCHERS have concluded that oregano should be called a flavor instead of a particular herb, as so many plants contain the characteristic oregano essential oils. In Mexico, a number of oreganos are used to flavor foods, the most popular of which is *Lippia graveolens,* which is also the one you are most apt to purchase in Mexican grocery stores north of the border. Mexican oreganos are available from specialty nurseries in the United States. Varieties of the European oreganos can be substituted for Mexican oregano. Greek oregano *(Origanum vulgare ssp. hirtum)* is an excellent substitution.

The Mexican oreganos, both tender perennials hardy only to USDA Zone 8, are fairly tall, woody plants with a rangy growth habit. *Lippia graveolens* is widely grown in Mexico, with *Poliomentha longiflora* usually found only in certain regions.

Mexican oregano

How to grow: Plant Mexican oreganos in full sun in a light, fast-draining soil. To assure the best flavor, start plants from transplants or cuttings, not seeds. To encourage new succulent growth, cut plants back in late spring and again in midsummer. Except in very sandy soils or in containers, moderate watering and little or no fertilizing keeps plants healthy. Root rots are a common problem in clay soils and in containers. Spider mites are occasional problems in hot weather and when plants are grown inside.

Varieties

Generic *Lippia graveolens* is carried by Native Seeds/SEARCH, Richters, and Well-Sweep Herb Farm. Generic *Poliomentha longiflora* is carried by Well-Sweep Herb Farm.

How to prepare: In Mexico, oregano is almost always used in its dried form. For traditional uses of the Mexican oreganos, add the leaves to chili dishes and salsa; use in fillings for burritos, tamales, and chiles rellenos; and apply as seasoning to such seafood dishes as stuffed fish and ceviche, such meat dishes as pork stew (see recipe, page 87), and to the famous tripe soup, *menudo*. In many parts of Mexico, the leaves are toasted in a dry comal or skillet before using. Both Mexican oreganos can be air-dried by hanging in a warm dry place as well dried in a dehydrator or microwave oven.

PEPPERS
(CHILES: HOT PEPPERS; MORRONES: BELL PEPPERS)
Capsicum spp.

IT'S IMPOSSIBLE TO IMAGINE Mexican cooking without chiles, which have added their delightful spiciness and deep flavors to Mexican cooking since about 7500 B.C. Nowhere else in the world is there such appreciation for not just the heat but the different flavors inherent in the individual types. From eons of experience, Mexicans have selected chiles they prefer in the green stage, others they like red and ripe, and yet others that are primarily eaten dried. Further, while some peppers, like the jalapeño and the poblano, are popular in most regions, some, like the habañero, are most associated with only one locale—in this case, the Yucatán.

Some of the most traditional chiles grow poorly in northern latitudes. Information in seed catalogs and with the following varieties listed note such limitations.

'Jalapeño Freinza'

In basket, clockwise from top: 'Manzano,' 'Chile d'Arbol,' orange habañero, jalapeño, poblano, and serranos in the center. *(Above)* green and red-ripe serranos.

How to grow: Peppers are tender perennials that tolerate no frost so are usually grown as warm-weather annuals. Start seeds indoors 8 to 10 weeks before you plan to set them out in the garden. Plant pepper seeds about $1/4$ inch deep and 1 inch apart. Keep the seed bed moist but not soggy; locate in a warm place. Best results are gained by using propagation mats under the seedling trays. Once seedlings have two sets of true leaves, move them up to 4-inch pots. When these peppers are about 4 inches tall and have several sets of leaves—and the weather is reliably warm—they can be transplanted into the garden, about 2 feet apart. Keep the transplants moist but not soggy for the first few weeks.

Peppers need warmth, full sun (except in extremely hot areas, where some afternoon shade is best), and a well-drained, moderately rich soil with a pH between 6.0 and 8.0. Most garden soils need the addition of compost and well-aged manure, a phosphorus source such as rock phosphate or bone meal, and kelp meal to provide trace minerals and potassium.

After the first fruit sets, apply a balanced organic vegetable fertilizer. Do not overfertilize with nitrogen, as too much favors leaf growth over the formation of flowers and fruits.

Peppers need regular watering, but most pepper problems are caused by overwatering or poor drainage. A thick organic mulch can increase your pepper yield. In some cool, short-season areas, a black plastic mulch is often used to warm the soil. (See "Mulching" in Appendix A.) Most pepper plants benefit from staking.

Most pepper problems are cultural rather than related to pests or diseases. When pods drop prematurely, it's due to heat stress, lack of sufficient water, or too much nitrogen. Crop rotation deters the buildup of pests and diseases. (See "Crop Rotation" in Appendix A.) Fusarium and verticillium wilt are possible disease problems.

Once peppers get near full size, you can pick them at any color stage. Cut, rather than pull, the peppers.

Seed saving: Peppers may self-pollinate or they may be insect pollinated—resulting in cross-pollination. Hot peppers cross much more readily than sweet. To assure purity, grow only one variety or cover the plants with floating row covers to restrict insect activity. In this event, you should hand pollinate the peppers for the best fruit set.

To gather seeds, harvest the fruits when they are just slightly overripe and beginning to wither. Select peppers just past the point you'd want to eat them. The fruits, however, shouldn't be rotting. Generally speaking, ripe peppers are red in color. Exceptions are numerous, however. To collect the seeds, you can spoon them out or cut the stem end of the pepper off and tap the seeds free. You'll probably want to wear gloves when working with hot peppers. Dry seeds for about 2 weeks, then store for next year.

Capsicum annuum

Be aware that, over the centuries, the names of many Mexican peppers have become a muddle. For instance, the identical dark green, wedge-shaped pepper is called ancho, pasilla, or poblano depending on how and where it is being used. In most of Mexico, where it evolved, it is called a poblano when it is in its fresh state and an ancho when dried. In the United States, when you order seeds in most catalogs, this pepper is designated an ancho, but when you buy the same pepper fresh in most markets, it is called a poblano—except in parts of California, where it might be called a pasilla. The true Mexican pasillas, however, appear wrinkled and dark brown when ripe and exude a raisinlike aroma.

Varieties

Gardeners in northern climates are most successful if they choose varieties from seed companies such as Nichols Garden Seeds, Johnny's Selected Seeds, and Territorial Seed Company that specialize in short, cool-season varieties.

'Ancho Mulatto' ('Mulato'): very dark brown when ripe; large, to 5 inches long and 3 inches across; fairly spicy, great flavor; used for stuffing and drying; not adapted to northern gardens. Related pepper 'Mulato Isleno' bred for Northwest; carried by Nichols Garden Nursery

Ancho/Poblano: 80 days; dark green, pear-shaped fruits; rich, meaty, essence-of-pepper flavor; one of the best; use roasted when fresh; called ancho when dried; not for cool-summer areas

'Cascabel': 90 days; very pungent; dark green to reddish brown; round 1-inch pods; usually used dried; grows best in Southwest

'Chili de Arbol' ('de Arbol,' Tree chili): Mexican people consider this to be among the best of the very hot peppers; similar to Cayennes; fruits are 2 1/2 inches long by 1/2 inch wide; pods are light green when immature and red when ripe; upright plants grow to 6 feet; not adapted to northern gardens but can be grown as houseplants

Jalapeño: 75 days; small, hot, thick-walled fruits of variable flavor depending on the seed company; best when green, ripens to red; called cuaresmeños in Mexico

'Jalapeño Frienza': 67 days; early; dark green to bright red; large, to 3 1/2 inches long; medium hot; high yields; 2 feet tall; fruits all season; good for short seasons

'Mexican Negro' ('Chile Negro'): pasilla type; pods 6 inches long, 1 1/2 inch wide; mildly pungent, rich fruity flavor; dark brown when ripe; for drying; best in Southwest

'Pizza Pepper': 80 days; fruits are thick-walled, flavorful, very mild; early, prolific; jalapeño type developed for the Northwest

Serrano: 80 days; 2 inches long; green to red; rich, hot flavor; 3 feet tall, upright plants; among the most popular of the fresh chile peppers used in Mexico; green when immature, ripening to red, and used in both stages

'Super Serrano': hot; best serrano for northern gardens; available from Johnny's Selected Seeds

Capsicum annuum
var. aviculare (bird peppers)

The term *bird peppers* is often used when referring to various small-podded wild and domesticated species of peppers, including those of *C. annuum* var. *aviculare*. The pods are tiny and fiery hot. The seeds are slow to germinate (from 3 to 12 weeks) and the plants need a long, hot growing season of 90 to 200 days to mature the fruits. They may, however, be grown in containers and brought inside in winter or grown in greenhouses.

The best known of these are called chiltepíns. (According to Dr. Paul Bosland, pepper researcher at New Mexico State University, the word *chiltepín* is usually used to refer to the small round-podded peppers, and the word *chilipiquín* is commonly used to refer to the pointed peppers.) These are some of the hottest peppers grown, measuring between 50,000 to 100,000 on the Scoville Heat Units Scale.

Varieties of chiltepíns are named for the region where the seed was collected. Native Seeds/SEARCH has a large selection of chiltepíns.

Chitlepín

Varieties

Chiltepín (tepin, chiltepin): green to red, usually round, though some are elongated; plants average 4 feet; available from Redwood City, Tomato Growers, and Native Seeds/SEARCH

Chilipiquín (piquin, pequin): green to red, elongated ½-inch pods (up to 3 inches on plants in home gardens); available from Redwood City, J. L. Hudson, and The Pepper Gal

Capsicum chinense

While the name means "from Havana," habañeros are commonly grown on the Yucatán Peninsula.

Varieties

'Habañero': 100 days; 1 to 2 ½ inches long, 1 inch wide; green ripening to true orange; extremely hot, use carefully; moderately successful in most northerly gardens

Capsicum frutescens

C. frutescens need warm, long summers to produce well. The plants hold their 3-inch narrow pods, erect. The fruits are yellow, purple, or green, ripening to red. They are hot, rated between 55,000 and 80,000 Scoville Heat Units. In the United States, the most commonly known *C. frutescens* is the 'Tabasco' pepper, of Louisiana Tabasco sauce fame. The name, though, comes from where these peppers hail— Tabasco, Mexico. 'Tabasco' peppers, which in Mexico are also often sold as simply "red chiles," are one of the few peppers that produce well in Florida all summer long.

'Habañero' *(above);* 'Tabasco' *(middle);* and 'Mazano' *(below)*

Varieties

'Greenleaf Tabasco': 80 days; resistant to tobacco etch virus; now used to make Tabasco sauce; best for the South and East

'Tabasco': 80 days; fiery hot; light yellow green ripening to red; originally used to make Tabasco sauce; tall plants

Capsicum pubescens

The round pods of *C. pubescens* are about 3 inches long and 2 inches across. Coming from high mountain country, the plants require cooler weather than most peppers, though they won't survive hard freezes. They need a moderate climate with a long growing season plus bees and another plant of the same variety to be pollinated and produce fruit, or they must be hand pollinated.

Varieties

'Rocoto' ('Manzano'): 90 to 180 days; very hot, looks like a small apple; orange; best in mild coastal or mountainous areas

How to prepare: Mexican cooks have many techniques for preserving and cooking with chiles. I cover most of the basics, including drying, roasting, and making chipotles in "Cooking from the Mexican Garden" on pages 61–89. Here, I am most interested in the flavors of the different types of chiles and suggestions for their specific uses in traditional Mexican meals.

Ancho/poblano peppers are beloved in Mexico and are my favorite, too. They are used fresh when green, most often roasted to develop their rich flavor and remove their tough skin. Once peeled, they can be stuffed with cheese or meat for rellenos and can be cut up and used in vegetable dishes, stews, cooked sauces, and chili. Strips of roasted poblano peppers (called *rajas*) are stewed in sour cream (see recipe, page 68), wrapped with cheese in a warm tortilla for a heavenly snack, and added to burritos, tamales, and tacos. They are added to *arroz verde* (green rice), where they are combined with chicken broth and cilantro, stewed with *nopalitos* (cactus pads) and pork, and often used in a traditional mole.

When ripe, the poblanos are dried. The dried pepper, then usually called an ancho, is toasted and then reconstituted in hot water and ground to a paste for the basis of numerous traditional Mexican salsas and stews, including tortilla soup (see recipe, page 76), red pozole (see recipe, page 78), and chicken or turkey moles.

In Mexico, green, raw jalapeños are popular chopped and used fresh in salsas, quesadillas, burritos, and tacos. Because the fruits are fleshy, jalapeños don't dry well unless they are smoked. Pickled jalapeños are commonly offered on the table so diners can help themselves. Smoked jalapeños are called chipotles; see the information on smoking jalapeños on page 66. When preserved in a tomato sauce, they are called chipotles en adobo. Chipotles are made from both green and red jalapeños. Ground chipotle peppers add a smoky, rich flavor as well as heat to roast meat, marinades, and sauces.

In Mexico, serranos are most commonly used in their green stage. They are quite hot and wonderful used fresh in really spicy salsas, guacamole, and

(In basket, clockwise from top) 'Guajillo,' 'Cascabel,' chile ancho, pequins, pasilla

cooked dishes including chili, eggs, beans, and other vegetable dishes. They can also be pickled or dried, as they are fairly thin walled. Dried serranos may be ground for use in chili powder. I've had serranos served to me on a little plate to accompany a taco or burrito; they were quickly fried in a little oil and had lots of flavor. In Mexico, pickled serranos are sometimes served with pickled onions and carrots to accompany beer.

'Chili de Arbol' is a lovely, complex pepper that is very spicy and used fresh or dried with meats, in chili, in salsas—whenever a dish calls out for a very hot pepper.

Despite their size, chiltepíns and chilipiquíns pack a real wallop and should be used only when a very hot pepper is desired. The pods are usually dried, then ground into powder. (Use a mask and grind them outside or they will seriously affect your eyes and breathing.) Sometimes they are com-

bined with a milder but flavorful chile, such as ancho. They can also be used in hot sauces or crushed and used with beans or in soups and stews.

Habañeros are hotter still and I wear gloves when preparing them to avoid burning my hands. Small amounts of the minced peppers are added raw to fresh tomato salsas in the Yucatán, where they are most popular. People in this region enjoy habañeros with seafood and in ceviches as well.

'Rocotos' are flavorful, somewhat spicy, chiles used fresh in salsas or stuffed and baked. They have thick walls and do not dry well.

49

PRICKLY PEAR
(NOPALES)
Opuntia spp. *(Nopalea* spp.)

PRICKLY PEAR CACTUS IS AN evergreen, herbaceous perennial. The flat, bristly pads or paddles (actually the stems) are called *nopales* or *nopalitos* in Mexico, where they are cooked and eaten as a popular green vegetable. Most prickly pear species are large, to 15 feet, and have showy yellow blossoms and yellow or purple fruits, some of which are tasty.

How to grow: The cultivation of cacti is different than that of other kinds of plants. Here are the basics:

Some species are hardy to around 20°F but most are much less hardy and are brought indoors in cold areas. If you are able to get a pad from a friend's plant or from the market, let the cut portion dry for a few days, then place it right side up in slightly damp sand. If starting with seeds, plant them $1/2$ inch deep in good planting mix. Keep barely moist and out of the sun. The germination can take 6 months.

Once plants are established, they need full sun, average soil, and extremely good drainage. Prickly pears grown in the ground take care of themselves after the first year but need occasional watering the first summer. If you grow them in containers, feed with cactus food and water infrequently. Prickly pear cacti have few pests and diseases.

Harvest young pads, as older pads get tough and fibrous. Irritating bristles grow all over most species. Wear leather gloves when harvesting both fruits and pads.

Varieties
When purchasing plants or seeds, be aware that not all *Opuntia* species are prickly pear; some belong to a group called *jumping cholla* and are not good for eating. Edible *Opuntia* are available from some specialty local nurseries and

Prickly pear cactus pads ready for harvest.

mail-order sources listed in the Resources section.

While, technically, any flat-padded *Opuntia* can be used for nopales, some species have tenderer pads or fewer spines. Hardy *Opuntias* tend to be small (with pads 3 to 4 inches in diameter) and more fibrous than less hardy types. Some varieties are best grown for fruits, others for their pads.

Opuntia cochenillifera (Nopalea cochenillifera): often called the true 'Nopal'; fruits and pads are edible; flowers rose-colored; grows to 15 feet with huge pads; tender; available from Mesa Garden

O. ficus-indica (Indian fig): one of the most common; usually considered best for fruits; yellow flowers; grows to 15 feet; some spineless ones are offered (Burbank's Spineless is a widely used generic name); available from Chiltern Seeds

O. compressa (O. humifusa, O. vulgaris): many-branched plant, usually prostrate; small pads; yellow flowers; grown from Massachusetts to Montana, south to Florida; plants from Goodwin Creek Gardens and Midwest Cactus

O. robusta (Dinner plate): to 6 feet; large, edible circular pads; fruits are deep red; from central Mexico; hardy to Zone 9; seeds available from Hurov's Seeds & Botanicals

O. streptacantha (Tuna cardona): grows to 15 feet; spiny round pads to 12 inches; common source of nopalitos; yellow flowers; edible fruits are red or yellow; from Mexico; seeds available from Hurov's Seeds & Botanicals

Using gloves, remove the spines of the prickly pear pad with a knife. Cut or slice into dice for cooking.

How to prepare: The young pads of the prickly pear cactus are covered with bristles that must be removed before eating. (Some are so small as to be invisible.) To remove, wear gloves and, holding the paddle by the stem end, use a sharp knife to slice off the outside edges. Then cut the tops off the spiny ridges, leaving most of the skin intact. Next, cut the pads into strips or small squares and boil them for about 25 minutes or until tender. Rinse the boiled nopales for 5 to 10 minutes under running water to remove the slippery juices. They can be reheated in a little butter, salt, and pepper, and served as a side dish (the taste most closely resembles that of string beans, but is unique). More often, they are made into a salad (see recipe, page 74), added to soups, or combined with seasonings in scrambled eggs served with tortillas. Nopales take well to all sorts of seasonings and can be sautéed with onions and chiles or added to a pork stew as well.

Prickly pear fruits are plum-shaped, 1 ½ to 3 inches long; the bristly hairs are removed before eating by rubbing them with canvas. Their lush red pulp looks like watermelon. Some species have orange or yellow flesh. The pulp is sweet but also extremely seedy, so it is eaten with care. Prickly pear fruits are usually served as a fresh fruit, well chilled, or pickled.

RADISHES
(RÁBANOS)
Raphanus sativus

WHILE NOT NATIVE, RED radishes are common in Mexico.

How to grow: Sow radish seeds directly in the garden after the last frost or sow them in early fall. Plant seeds ¼ inch deep and thin to 2 inches apart. They can be planted in rows or wide beds. The soil should be light and well drained, with a generous amount of compost. Radishes are light feeders and need little fertilizer. Keep radishes consistently moist to avoid cracking and a too-hot taste.

In some areas of the country, radishes are bothered by root maggots, which are best controlled by crop rotation. Flea beetles can also be a problem.

Generally speaking, radishes should be harvested when they are about the size of large cherries. If they are left in the ground too long they have a tendency to get hot and fibrous.

Varieties

'Crimson Giant': 28 days; very large, deep crimson round globes; crisp and sweet; not pithy

'Early Scarlet Globe': 23 days; 1-inch, globe-shaped roots; mild, sweet flavor

'Sparkler': 24 days; round, red, white tipped; crisp, tender white flesh

How to prepare: Radishes are most commonly used as a garnish. Slice the roots in thin coins and either put them directly on the dish being garnished or, more traditionally, offer them with a host of other flavoring garnishes—salsa, chopped onions, fried chile strips, and such—so diners can season the dish themselves.

'Sparkler' radish

SQUASH
(CALABAZA)
SUMMER SQUASH
Cucurbita pepo

WINTER SQUASH
Cucurbita spp.

SQUASH IS NATIVE TO MEXICO, where the fruits, seeds, and flowers play different roles in the cuisine. Recipes using summer squash are much more common than those made with winter squash, which is referred to as pumpkin. When it comes to winter squash, the blossoms and seeds are the stars.

How to grow: All squash, summer or winter, are warm-season annuals. In short-summer areas, seeds must be started indoors. The plants are usually grown in hills, two plants to a hill. Space hills 6 feet apart for summer squash and up to 10 feet apart for winter squash and pumpkins. If direct seeding, plant seed somewhat more thickly and later thin to the above distances. All squash need full sun, rich organic soil with added chicken manure, and ample water during the growing season. They benefit from monthly applications of fish emulsion.

Squash bugs, spotted and striped cucumber beetles, and (east of the Rockies) squash vine borers may cause problems. Expect mildew by the end of the season in most climates.

Pick summer squash after the blossoms have withered or as long as the squash are still tender. It is important to keep excess summer squash picked

Striped chilacayote-type squash and 'Pink Banana Jumbo' *(above);* and numerous types of edible pumpkn seeds *(below)*

or the plant drastically slows its production.

Unlike summer varieties, winter squash and pumpkins are usually picked when fully mature. When fully ripe, the rinds of most are hard and the exterior color highly saturated. Leave about 2 inches of stem attached or the squash is likely to rot.

To harvest the flowers, try to gather blossoms in the early morning before they close and put their bases or stems in water in the refrigerator until you need them. The female flowers have an immature little squash at the base where they meet the stem; the male flowers end at the stem. Most gardeners gather only male blossoms, making

'Grey Zucchini' and petunias

sure to leave a few to pollinate the females. To slow down summer squash production or thin a winter squash, harvest females too. In Mexico, the bright orange pumpkin and winter squash blossoms are preferred over the paler, greenish zucchini flowers.

Varieties

Mexican cooks prefer pale or dark green zucchini over yellow; round varieties are common.

Summer Squash

'**Grey Zucchini**': 42 days; bush; medium green with gray specks, fruits to 12 inches long; fine-quality flesh

'**Ronde De Nice**': 55 days, bush; tender, light green skin, round fruits

Winter Squash

Native Seeds/SEARCH carries several cushaw squashes from Mexico, most of which take an extended warm season to mature. In addition, try some of these varieties:

'**Chilacayote**': *Cucurbita ficifolia;* a tender perennial that spreads hundreds of feet; in a long growing season it produces large, watermelon-shaped green-and-white striped squashes; young squash are cooked like summer squash, almost-mature fruits are cooked with sugar to make a candylike sweet; also grown just for the black seeds, which are oily and nutritious; carried by J. L. Hudson in their Zapotec Collection

'**Green-Striped Cushaw**' ('**Striped Crookneck**'): 110 days; vining; 10-pound fruits, creamy white skins with green stripes; slightly sweet, yellow flesh; resistant to squash vine borer

'**Pink Banana Jumbo**': 105 days; fruits to 4 feet long; turns pink at maturity; light orange flesh; carried by R. H. Shumway's and Willhite Seed Company; Burpee carries a bush version with smaller fruits

'**Santa Domingo Cushaw**': 110 days; large green squash with white flesh

and tan seeds; large vines; can be eaten as a summer squash when young; 18 inches or so; can be made into a sweet; carried by Abundant Life

'**Tamala de Carne**': large buff-colored fruits with variable shapes; bright orange, juicy flesh; grows best in hot weather; carried by J. L. Hudson in their Zapotec Collection

'**Triple Treat**': 110 days, a bright orange small pumpkin; best for pies; great for pumpkin seeds; available from Burpee

How to prepare: In Mexico, summer squash are often used in soups (see recipe, page 77) and are the perfect vehicle for absorbing the flavors of chiles, garlic, onion, tomato, and numerous herbs such as epazote, oregano, and thyme. A representative dish might include cubed, sautéed pork with garlic, tomatoes or tomatillos, green onions, and chiles, served with corn tortillas.

Winter squash are offered in Mexican markets but one seldom sees a recipe for them. I've seen some reference to it being cubed and used in soups and stews, and I know it is used as a filling for sweet empanadas (pastries similar to turnovers and popular in Mexican bakeries). The 'Banana' squash and the large green and white squash called chilacayote are often stewed with large amounts of sugar and offered in markets as a candy (*dulce*). Mexican cooking authority Nancy Zaslavsky mentioned preparing the white-fleshed chilacayote by cooking and combined with sweetening to make a cooling drink.

On the other hand, the seeds of winter squash, usually called pumpkin, are common ingredients in Mexican cooking. They are enjoyed whole as a snack, either plain or salted, or are hulled and added to a candy similar to peanut brittle. The seeds are hard to hull; hit them with a mallet and sort out the pieces of kernels. (Hulled seeds can be purchased from Mexican markets and natural food stores.) The hulled seeds are most popular in moles, where they both thicken and season the sauce. The seeds are sometimes ground with the hulls for a less greasy but more textured sauce.

Squash blossoms, too, contribute to Mexican cuisine. Pumpkin and winter squash blossoms (known as *calabacitas criollas* or *flores de calabaza*) are most often used, but summer squash and zucchini blossoms are also used and are much more common north of the border. Chopped squash flowers are added to quesadillas fillings (see recipe, page 83) and soups with corn and chiles; they are also fried, grilled, and stuffed with many types of fillings themselves.

Squash blossoms have a slightly sweet nectar taste. To prepare the flowers, wash and gently dry them. (Watch out for bees if you are using closed blossoms; they sometimes get trapped inside and, contrary to reason, are not happy when you free them!) If you're using the blossoms for fritters or stuffing, keep the stems on. Otherwise, remove stems, stamens, and stigmas.

TOMATILLOS
(TOMATES VERDES, TOMATES DE CASCAR)
Physalis ixocarpa

THIS VEGETABLE IS RELATED TO and somewhat resembles a small green tomato, but it has a tangy flavor and a paperlike husk.

How to grow: Tomatillos are annuals that are started and grown much as tomatoes are (see page 56). The plants grow more quickly and tend to be smaller than most tomatoes, though rangier and more brittle. They are usually grown without support or cages. Space transplants to 3 feet apart. Branch tips can be pinched back to control ranginess. Plants tend to be prolific producers and relatively free of pests and disease. Harvest when the paper husk loosens, just before the fruit begins to turn pale yellow.

Varieties
'De Milpa' ('Purple De Milpa'): 70 days; small (fruits are 1 1/2 inches across) but considered one of the best flavored; fruits blush with purple after harvest; keeps well

'Toma Verde' ('Large Green'): 65 days; large green fruits 2 to 3 inches across; mild; easy to husk; good quality; not pithy when ripe

How to prepare: Before using tomatillos, remove the paperlike husks and rinse lightly. They are used raw or, more often, cooked. To cook, put in a pot, cover with water, and simmer for about 5 to 10 minutes, then proceed with your choice of a number of recipes. For a more mellow and fuller flavor, husk and roast tomatillos on a comal until browned and slightly mushy when blended. Stew tomatillos with chiles, onions, and pork (see recipe, page 85), which complement their tart, slightly tomatolike flavor. Probably the most popular way to serve them is in *salsa verde* (see recipe, page 71), the condiment, and in the sauce for *enchiladas verdes* with garlic, chiles, and cilantro.

'De Milpa' and 'Toma Verde' tomatillos

TOMATOES

(JITOMATES, TOMATE)

Lycopersicon esculentum

JUICY, RIPE TOMATOES ARE celebrated in Mexican cooking. They are native to the area, having been domesticated over 2,000 years ago in Mexico and Central America.

How to grow: Tomatoes are heat-loving plants. Though perennials, they are grown as warm-weather annuals, as they tolerate no frost. Extreme heat can sunburn the fruits, though, so protect them in extremely hot climates. Many varieties, especially the big slicing, heirloom beefsteak types, will not set fruits well in temperatures in the high 90s (or below 50°F, either). Start plants from seed about 6 to 8 weeks before your last frost, planting them 1/4 inch deep in good potting soil. Keep the plants in a very sunny window or under grow lights. When all danger of frost is over and the plants are about 6 inches high, transplant them in the garden, about 4 feet apart, in full sun and in a well-drained soil amended with a good amount of organic matter. Plant the transplants deep—the soil should come up to the first set of new leaves. At transplant time and again when the fruits are beginning to set, fertilize the plants with fish meal, chicken manure, or a premixed low-nitrogen, high-phosphorus organic fertilizer formulated for tomatoes. A form of calcium may be needed to prevent blossom-end rot, though keeping

the watering consistent usually controls it. Liming may be needed every few years if you live in an acid-soil area, as tomatoes prefer a soil pH around 6.5. Most gardeners prefer to stake or trellis tomatoes. These supports help your plants to take up less room and keep the fruit from spoiling on the ground. Deep, fairly infrequent waterings are best. Mulch with compost after the soil has warmed thoroughly.

A few major pests afflict tomatoes, including tomato hornworms, cutworms, tobacco budworms, nematodes, and whiteflies. A number of diseases are fairly common to tomatoes, including early and late blight, fusarium and verticillium wilt, alternaria, and tobacco mosaic. Control disease by rotating crops and planting resistant varieties. The capital-letter abbreviation sometimes included after a name gives an indication of the disease resistance. For example, VF or VFF indicates the variety is resistant to some strains of verticillium and fusarium wilt. Other such codes are N, for nematodes, T or TMV for tobacco mosaic virus, and A, for alternaria.

Harvest tomatoes as they ripen. Color and a slight give to the fruit are the best guides to ripeness. Harvest with a slight twist of the wrist or with scissors. Do not refrigerate tomatoes unless they are dead ripe or the flavor deteriorates.

Seed saving: Tomatoes are susceptible to numerous diseases. To avoid contaminated seed, your seed sources should be the finest fruits from your best nondiseased plants. Pick these

fruits just a day or two past fully ripe. Place mashed tomato pulp and seeds together in a glass jar with about 1/3 cup water. Allow the mixture to ferment at room temperature for 4 days or until obviously moldy. Stir the mixture on the first and third days and skim off floating pulp and seeds on the second and fourth days and discard. Retain the seeds that sink to the bottom of the brew. Rinse them with clear water, spread them out on a glass dish, and let them dry for a week. Place them in airtight containers for winter storage.

Varieties

Tomato varieties are either determinate or indeterminate. Determinate plants grow little or not at all once the fruit is set and the fruits ripen within a short period of time. Indeterminate vines continue to grow and fruit all season. They need staking.

'Costoluto Genovese': 80 days; indeterminate; slightly tart; large, red, deeply fluted; productive vines; resistant to verticillium and fusarium wilt

'Beefsteak': 80 days; indeterminate; large, slightly ribbed red fruits up to 2 pounds; excellent slicer; meaty and delicious; available on some Mexican market seed racks in the Southwest

'Oxheart': 80 days; indeterminate; heirloom; large, heart-shaped pink fruits, up to 2 pounds

'Red Calabash': ruffled, fairly small red fruits; probably from the state of Chiapas; available from Seeds of Change

'Roma': 75 days; determinate; widely

'Costoluto Genovese' tomatoes

adapted standard paste tomato; great for Mexican sauces; some disease resistance; productive; 'Roma VF' has more disease resistance

'Zapotec Pleated' ('Zapotec Ribbed'): 80 days, large ruffled pink to red tomato; hollow cavity; from Oaxaca; available from Seeds of Change

How to prepare: Tomatoes are beloved in Mexico and used in a great many classic dishes. Chopped, raw tomatoes find their way into fresh salsas, tacos, tortas (sandwiches), and burritos; are combined with nopalitos (see recipe, page 74) or jícama in salads; and are used as a garnish for soups and pozole. Tomatoes are most often used cooked, often as the first step in a typical puréed "fried sauce." For centuries, tomatoes have been charred and blistered on a comal over a fire or grill, then peeled and ground for a roasted salsa (see recipe, page 71) or as the basis for red pozole, pork stew, and tortilla soup (see recipes, page 76). For more on roasting tomatoes, see page 67. Tomatoes are usually added to menudo (tripe soup), a national dish, and to cooked sauces for huevos rancheros, tamales, enchiladas, and casseroles (see the basic sauce recipe on page 69). Tomatoes are included in flavored rice dishes and cooked with all sorts of greens and other vegetables, including boiled potatoes, chiles, fava beans (see recipe, page 81), and zucchini.

WILD GREENS

(QUELITES)

MALVA

Malva sylvestris var. *mauritiana, M. verticillata*

PURSLANE (VERDOLAGAS, PIGWEED)

Portulaca oleracea var. *sativa*

THERE'S BEEN A REBIRTH OF interest in wild greens in the last few years as food historians and nutritionists look to how cultures have fed themselves throughout history. What they have discovered is that these foraged greens (often considered weeds by the greater population) are especially nutritious, filled with vitamins, minerals, and antioxidants. Fortunately, in most countries, a number of folks keep the practice of foraging going and can identify the plants and explain their preparation and medicinal benefits.

Many wild greens grow in Mexico—some native, others introduced—but few of them are available to gardeners north of the border. The exceptions are some of the amaranths and the huauzontli, discussed earlier, and purslane. The latter is so popular in Mexico (and in France) that seeds are readily available in the United States. In addition, a number of malva species are commonly utilized in Mexico; while the exact species is not available here, two similar plants can be used as substitutes in recipes. For those traveling to Mexico there are

Green Purslane

more wild greens to explore, especially lamb's-quarters *(Chenopodium album)*, which is a common weed in the United States, and chepil *(Crotalaria longirostrata)*, a member of the pea family. It grows in corn fields in southern Mexico.

Before you start enjoying wild greens, however, you need to get a good weed-identification guide or wild edible plant book so that you can properly identify the correct genus and species and avoid toxic plants.

Purslane

Purslane is a tangy green with a slippery texture and lots of omega-3 fatty acids, so good for our hearts and immune systems. The domesticated variety is popular in many parts of the world. The wild form is a low-growing fleshy herb that most gardeners know as a pest—one of many weeds called pigweed.

How to grow: Gardeners don't plant the wild purslane; it just shows up. To grow the more succulent cultivated purslane in your garden, obtain seeds from specialty herb nurseries listed in the Resources section. Start the seeds of these fast-growing annual plants in good garden soil in spring after the weather warms. Sow seeds a few inches apart and thin to 6 inches apart, or grow in a cold frame in spring and fall. To produce succulent leaves, keep the plants well watered and cut back often to force new growth. Harvest young shoots and tender leaves in 60 days. Remove flower stalks as they form or they will be tough and go to seed.

Varieties

'Golden' ('Golden Leaf'): large, succulent golden tinged leaves; carried by Richters Herbs and J. L. Hudson

'Green' ('Green Leaf'): green succulent plants; carried by Richters Herbs and J. L. Hudson

How to prepare: The weedy purslane has a stronger flavor then the domesticated variety and less should be used in a recipe. Add purslane to pork stew (see recipe, page 87), to simple soups (see recipe, page 77), or combine it with other vegetables in a tomato sauce and use it for a filling for tortillas.

Malva

Like purslane, malvas also have a mucilaginous quality similar to okra. I've been told that in some parts of Mexico a malva soup is consumed as a first course before a rich meal to prepare the stomach for what follows.

Two edible domesticated malvas are available from seed companies that can be substituted for the Mexican species.

How to grow: Malvas are easy to grow and tolerate most soils, though they prefer well-drained soil and cool temperatures. Sow seeds in early spring in the garden where they are to grow, in full sun or light shade in hot climates. Cover seeds just lightly with soil. Thin to 12 to 24 inches apart. (Seeds can be started indoors about 6 to 8 weeks before planting outside, if desired.) Water regularly. Cut the perennial malva back in the fall. For cooking or for use in salads, harvest malva leaves while still young and tender.

Varieties

Malva sylvestris **var.** *mauritiana*

'Zebra Mallow': a hardy perennial often grown as an annual; flowers are white to rosy purple with dark veins; plants 3 to 4 feet tall; carried by J. L. Hudson, which says that the flowers are edible and the young leaves are good in salads or boiled like greens

M. verticillata (M. crispa): annual or biennial; also called curled mallow; small round leaves with wavy ruffled margins; flowers are white or purple; carried by Abundant Life Seed Foundation

How to prepare: Cook the malvas the same way as amaranth and most other greens in Mexico are prepared—that is, briefly cooked with tomatoes or tomatillos and onions, garlic, and chiles. They, like their relative okra, also thicken soups and stocks and can be combined with other mild vegetables like zucchini to make a soothing soup sometimes taken to aid digestion; see the recipe on page 77.

Malva, one of many wild greens species in Mexico

cooking from the mexican garden

Mexican cuisine has its roots in the ancient Aztec civilization. When Cortés arrived in 1521, the native peoples in this part of the world were steeped in nature's bounty: corn, beans, tomatoes, squash, avocados, chilis, peanuts, turkey, a vast range of seafoods, and two indigenous delicacies—chocolate and vanilla. Montezuma, the last Aztec emperor, had lobsters, shrimp, quail, bananas, guavas, and pineapples brought to him from all over the country. A staple of the Aztecs was the tortilla, one of the world's most versatile foods. With the Spanish invasion, pork, beef, milk, wheat, sugar, onions, citrus, garlic, and numerous herbs and greens entered Mexico. Over the centuries, the foods of both cultures blended into a unique cuisine

Tamales, made from ground corn and seasoned with meats, vegetables, and chilis are a staple food in much of Mexico. Here, they are made with runner beans, red peppers, and winter squash.

Of course, the conquistadors affected cuisines in Europe as well by bringing home foods of the New World. The Italians embraced the tomato; the Germans, the potato; and the Swiss, chocolate. In turn, Mexican cooks found ways of using garlic, lime, cheese, pork, and beef. However, while North American cooking is basically European cooking adapted to New World ingredients, Mexican cuisine today can be traced directly to its pre-Hispanic origins. For this reason, those of us trained in any of the European-based cuisines come up against unfamiliar ingredients and techniques when we introduce our-

selves to Mexican cooking. For example, while many of us have made bread, few of us in the United States have actually made tortillas.

Mexican cooks use such ingredients as cinnamon, black pepper, and mint, as do cooks worldwide, but they use much more ground corn and chilis than do cooks in most other cultures. Within Mexico, we can discern regional characteristics as well, determined both by climatic and cultural factors. Avocado leaves and epazote are examples; these seasonings are used in the south but seldom appear in the north. Pinto beans are common in the north but black beans are the legume of choice in the south. Most North Americans are familiar with the foods of northern Mexico because of its proximity and because migration has been greater from that area, but the cuisines of the south are more connected to their Aztec roots and have much to offer.

To get a feel for Mexican cooking, we can describe general characteristics of the food. First, corn is almost always present in countless different forms. Also, many dishes take quite a bit of preparation time; in fact, two cooking steps are often involved. And the food tends to be generously seasoned.

What follows is an overall survey of the major vegetables used in Mexican cooking, a few cooking techniques, and a bit about some key ingredients. Once you master a few basics, such as making salsa, fixing a pot of creamy beans, and working with tortillas in various ways, you'll be able to prepare many a Mexican meal from your garden. These techniques, plus the recipes that follow, will take you a long way in exploring the rich relationship between garden-fresh vegetables and Mexico's distinctive cuisine.

Beans

Beans, primarily dry beans, are a staple in the Mexican diet. The dozens of varieties each differ subtly in both flavor and texture. The basic, traditional Mexican dry-bean dish is frijoles de olla, beans cooked very slowly and with very little seasoning. (Unlike north of the border, beans in Mexico are seldom cooked with meat, in such dishes as pork and beans.) Beans are served as a side dish or in soups, on tostadas or in tacos, tamales, and burritos. Black beans, with a sprig of epazote added toward the end of cooking, are most common in the Yucatán and central Mexico. In the Yucatán, cooks may

also add mint to the beans or sieve them to make a creamy purée. Beans are often refried with lard and garnished with cheese.

You probably have been taught to soak your dry beans overnight before cooking, but Mexican cooks quickly prepare their dried beans and I think they taste better and have a firmer texture. Try the Mexican way and you will be pleased.

Frijoles de Olla (Basic Beans)

The most traditional way to make this classic dish is to combine the first five ingredients and, when the beans are tender, add salt to taste and serve the beans as is. For a more complex dish, add the rest of the ingredients. The amount of liquid varies depending on whether you want a soup or a filling for tortillas. Either version can be served as side dish or used as a filling for tacos, tostadas, or burritos, or simply eaten by themselves with tortillas. These beans taste even better the next day.

1 pound (2 1/2 cups) dry beans
   (choose from pinto, pink, red,
   Peruano, tepary, black, or any
   good dry bean)
8 to 10 cups boiling water
2 tablespoons lard or bacon
   drippings
1 medium onion, chopped
3 cloves garlic, chopped
2 cups roasted, chopped tomatoes
   (skinned and seeded)
1 to 3 chopped serranos
1 poblano, roasted, peeled, and
   chopped
2 teaspoons ground cumin
2 large sprigs epazote (if using
   black beans)
Salt to taste
1/4 cup minced cilantro leaves
Mexican melting cheese or
   mozzarella (optional)

Place the first five ingredients in a large pot on low heat, cover, and cook for 1 to 2 hours or until beans are almost tender, stirring occasionally. (Cooking time varies greatly depending on the variety and freshness of the beans.) Add the tomatoes, chilis, cumin, and epazote (if using); cook for 1/2 hour longer, stirring frequently. If you like your beans soupy, then add a little boiling water; if thicker, cook them down. Fold in the cilantro. Serve the beans hot and garnished with cheese, if desired.

Serves 8 to 10.

Refried Beans

Refried beans are a staple in Mexico and one we could all use in our repertoire. I had problems making them until Luis Torres, friend and cooking maven, walked me through the process. He found I'd not been cooking the beans and oil long enough before mashing them. They were too firm to get smooth and velvety.

The thickness of the finished bean purée is a matter of taste. A thicker paste is good for burritos and tacos so they won't drip, but a moist, creamy product is great to accompany huevos rancheros. To change the consistency of your refried beans, add more or less bean liquid or water. Some cooks prefer to use more oil than is called for here; others like less.

1 pound dry pinto, Peruano, or
    black beans
1 to 3 cloves garlic
6 cups boiling water
1/2 cup corn oil or lard
1/2 to 1 teaspoon freshly ground
    cumin
Salt and freshly ground black
    pepper to taste

In a large pot, wash and sort through the beans and eliminate foreign matter and spoiled beans. Add garlic and water; bring back to the boil. Turn the heat to low and simmer beans for 1 to 1 1/2 hours or until tender. (Freshly harvested beans take less time than older ones.) Drain the beans and reserve the liquid.

Pour the oil in a large skillet. Turn the heat on high and carefully (they splatter) add drained beans and 1 1/4 cups of the bean liquid. Simmer, stirring occasionally, for 6 to 8 minutes or until the beans are fairly soft. Add more liquid if the beans are getting dry. Turn the heat down and mash them a little at a time with a potato masher. Again, add more bean liquid

if they get too dry. Add the cumin and salt and pepper, adjust the seasonings, and remove from heat. Serves 4 as a side dish.

Corn

Corn is Mexico's single most important food. There are large field corn varieties (mostly dent corn) for making hominy for tortillas and pozole; a smaller dent corn for roasting; and occasional sweet corns. The Mexican taste runs to chewy field corn for fresh corn, so it is starchier and possesses more corn taste than our sweet corns. It is used quite a bit—for example, in a fresh corn soup with tomatoes, onions, and garlic, and in tamales made from fresh corn scraped off the cob. A soup of fresh field corn, squash, and chilis is popular, as are vegetable soups with wheels of corn (the cob is cut in a few sections) so the diner can eat the kernels off the cob. Street vendors sell fresh corn on the cob, which their customers can dip in cream and season with grated cheese.

Corn on the Cob Mexican Style

Food vendors are a common sight in Mexico, even on the beach. They offer fruit, seafood appetizers, and corn on the cob—not just with butter and salt, but dipped in cream or painted with crema and dusted with cheese and powdered chilis.

3 ears of substantial, mature sweet
    corn or field corn, in the husk
1/4 cup heavy cream, warmed

3 tablespoons aged Mexican
cheese *(anejo)*, grated
Chili powder

Remove the husks from the corn but leave the stalk to use as a handle. Boil the corn for 6 to 8 minutes. Drain and place on a plate. Sprinkle a tablespoon or so of cream on each ear, turning it over to wet the entire cob. (In Mexico, people dip the ear of corn in a large container of warm cream.) Sprinkle 1 tablespoon of cheese on each ear and then dust with a little chili powder. Serves 3.

Dry Corn

Most of the corn consumed in Mexico is dry corn, used primarily in masa, a dough made from ground lime-treated kernels, a treatment referred to as hominying. Masa is most often formed into tortillas, which, in their versatility, resemble both bread and pasta. Tacos, for instance, are tortillas filled with meat and a little salsa. In Mexico, tortillas for tacos are usually soft, not crisp. Enchiladas are tortillas rolled around fillings of meat or cheese and covered with a sauce and cheese. Quesadillas are made with tortillas that are folded and stuffed with cheese, squash blossoms, cactus paddles, or other filling and then fried or cooked

on a griddle (see recipe, page 83). Tostadas are tortillas fried crisp and then topped with beans, chopped meat, salsa, lettuce, tomato, and cheese. With all those tortillas around, uses are found for the stale ones too—for instance, tortilla soups (see recipe, page 76) and casseroles (see recipe, page 85).

Tamales are another Mexican staple. These wonderful packets of masa dough and flavorings wrapped in corn husks or corn leaves are a fiesta staple. They can have fillings of all kinds—meat, poultry, seafood, beans, and chilis, not to mention the sweet tamales filled with fruits or sweet spiced beans and served for breakfast. In tropical regions, tamales are often wrapped in banana leaves rather than corn leaves or husks.

About Corn Tortillas

Warm corn tortillas are a classic part of most meals in Mexico, where tortillas are often either homemade or purchased a few times a day, still warm, from a local tortilla factory. Fresh tor-

tillas are soft and aromatic and eaten as we would eat bread at a meal, or they are wrapped around various fillings.

In the United States, commercial corn tortillas are most often found in plastic bags in grocery stores, either in the bread section or in the frozen food case. For fresh, hot tortillas, look for a nearby tortilla factory; these are increasingly popular and now found in many American metropolitan areas and most border towns.

Commercial tortillas need reheating. Many cooks warm corn tortillas, a dozen or so at a time, by wrapping them with a towel and steaming them in a metal or bamboo steamer basket for about 10 minutes or until the entire stack is hot. To keep them warm, they are put in a basket with a large napkin around them. My son-in-law, Joel Chavarin, introduced me to another method of heating tortillas I also enjoy. For crispier tortillas, I stack three or four on a hot comal and, with tongs, I keep rotating them from top to bottom until they are all warm and starting to turn golden in a few spots. I repeat the

process with more tortillas until I have enough. (I've also heated tortillas on a charcoal or gas grill, where they become a little more crisp and smoky tasting.) In Mexico, they serve eight to ten tortillas per person; north of the border, we generally eat fewer, say three or four each.

Because tortillas are so versatile, you can always put together a quick meal from the garden around them. Give me a batch of tortillas, a pot of beans, and some salsa (a garden staple I often put up), and I can take care of my meal planning for days. I serve warm tortillas rolled around refried beans and roasted chilis or chopped grilled onions, garnished with tomatoes and Mexican crema (similar to crème fraîche), one night, and maybe I put a little cooked chicken in tortillas with some cooked vegetables and cheese on another night. I might finish the week by cooking a mixture of zucchini, green peppers, onions, garlic, cumin, tomatoes, and grated cheese and serving it with tortillas and beans on the side.

Making Hominy Corn for Pozole

A soup called *pozole* is made with field corn (from large varieties called pozole corn), which can be grown in many parts of the United States. To prepare your corn for pozole, you must make it into hominy. To make hominy, you must purchase powdered slaked lime (calcium hydroxide). It's available from Mexican restaurants that make their own tortillas, and from tortilla factories. Ask for *cal*, its Spanish name.

Food-grade calcium hydroxide (slaked lime) is available from pharmacies.

Warning: Calcium hydroxide is a strong base solution and is sometimes sold as lye (lye being by definition any strong alkaline chemical). People have been known to hominy their corn with drain opener! The calcium hydroxide (or lye or slaked lime) which is sold in building supply stores and industrial outlets frequently contain unknown impurities and can be unsafe. Read the label—and be sure the calcium hydroxide you purchase is **food grade.**

I'm giving full directions here on processing pozole corn for soup only, as to make tortillas and tamales requires grinding the corn and few folks have the equipment. You may wish to consult Rick Bayless's cookbooks, which cover making tortillas and tamales in detail. Whether you are making pozole corn, tortillas, or tamales, the first process is the same; only the cooking and soaking times are different.

Rinse the corn and remove debris and damaged kernels. In a large enamel or stainless-steel pan, put 2 quarts of water and 2 1/2 tablespoons slaked lime; bring to a boil. Add about 4 cups of dried pozole corn and stir. Remove any floating empty kernels. To prepare pozole corn for soup, cook the corn for 12 to 14 minutes. Do not drain. Let the

corn soak for 3 or 4 hours. Next, rinse it 8 to 12 times under running water, using fresh water for each rinse. Rub the kernels between the palms of your hands to remove the remains of the skins. At this stage, you should have clean, fairly tender corn kernels, complete with the dark germ at the base of the kernel. For a fancy presentation, traditional cooks take the time to remove the germ so the kernels expand and look like flowers when they are cooked. I seldom have the patience for this, and I find it makes little difference on a day-to-day presentation. The corn, now treated with lime, is called *nixtamal*. Before making pozole, it is boiled for 3 or 4 hours or until tender. It is then combined with other ingredients for the soup. See the recipe on page 78.

Chilis

Chilis, of course, are used widely and distinctively in Mexican cooking. Here, their many flavors and subtleties reign. In the pepper entry in the Encyclopedia, I detail the primary Mexican chilis used in Mexico plus specific ways to use them. Here, I cover general cooking techniques and how to preserve and prepare chilis.

Most Mexican cooks prefer fresh chilies in their green rather than their red-ripe state. The ripe peppers are usually used dried. In a Mexican dish, the flavors of the chilis are as important as their hotness. Thus, for the average Mexican cook, the variety of chili used depends on the dish being prepared—

jalapeño, say, for salsa, and roasted poblano for rellenos. Another factor is geography. Thus, the habañero is preferred and used fresh or toasted in sauces in parts of the Yucatán, whereas the long, slim, black-green pasilla de Oaxaca is used for moles in Oaxaca. Neither is often seen in other areas of Mexico.

In Mexico, chilis are added fresh, roasted, powdered, or puréed to soups, stews, tortas (sandwiches), salsas, vegetable dishes, pickles, and most meat dishes. Chilis are generally added in the cooking process but they are also an ever-present condiment so diners can adjust the spiciness of their own dish. Pickled peppers, especially jalapeños, are common; briefly fried serranos (sauté whole green or red serranos in a little oil until they start to brown and soften) accompany tacos in many a *fonda* (market food stall); and small bowls of either chopped fresh chilis or a spicy salsa give diners many options.

Drying Chilis

Mexicans appreciate the deep, toasty flavors of dried chilis and use them in salsas, most soups and stews, and numerous appetizers. Because the flesh of the majority of hot peppers is thin, they are easy to dry. Further, some of the varieties arguably taste better in that form. One thick-walled pepper, the jalapeño, is also dried—in this case, by first smoking it. The smoked and dried jalapeño, called a chipotle, adds a lovely smoky flavor to sauces and soups.

To dry thin-walled peppers, first choose fully ripe, unblemished peppers. If you live in an arid climate, you can dry peppers on a screen in a warm dry place out of the sun and dew. Stir the peppers every day or so to promote even drying. If the peppers are large, they dry more readily if you cut a slit in the side. In rainy climates, or if the peppers are unripe, they must be dried in a dehydrator, in a gas oven using only the pilot light, or in an electric oven at 150°F for about 12 hours. Cut slits in the side of the peppers and rotate them occasionally. (The tiny bird peppers dry so readily they need only to be placed on a sunny windowsill for a few days.) Once your peppers are brittle, to keep them dry and the insects under control, store them in a jar with a lid or in a sealable freezer-strength plastic bag.

To bring out their rich flavors, dried chilis are often toasted on a hot comal for 30 seconds or until they release their perfume. To reconstitute the chilis, break them into a few pieces, put them in a bowl, pour hot water over them, and let them sit for 20 to 30 minutes before draining. For some recipes the water is retained and added to the recipe. The chilis can then be ground into a paste and added to sauces or combined with garlic and other spices to create a mole or salsa. (See the recipe for salsa cruda on page 71 for more information.)

How to Make Chipotles

Chipotles are smoked, dried jalapeño peppers. They look like wrinkled leather but are famous for their rich, smoky, complex flavors and their heat. A traditional way of preparing chipotles is to stew them in a mild red chili sauce. This flavorful mixture can be

added to numerous Mexican dishes. To use chipotles in a sauce, or a cooked dish, first toast, then soften them by pouring hot water over them and letting them sit for about 20 minutes. Cut the chipotles up or purée them and add the purée to your recipe. You can also grind dry chipotles into a powder that adds a smoky, hot dimension to food.

To smoke jalapeños, you need a smoker, commonly called a cajun cooker. A smoker is a metal box or cylinder that has a pan for charcoal at the bottom. Above the charcoal is a pan for water and above the water pan are racks for the chilis. Smokers are covered by a lid with a temperature gauge. Commercial smokers come with directions on basic smoking.

To make chipotles, half fill the pan in the bottom of the smoker with charcoal, light it, and burn until the charcoal is white hot. Once hot, place on top a few handfuls of mesquite shavings that were soaked in water for about 20 minutes. Fill the water pan and place it above the coals. Put green or red-ripe whole or halved jalapeños on the racks and cover the cooker. Smoke the jalapeños for 2 or 3 hours. You know when the smoker is working properly when the temperature gauge indicates you are in the ideal range. Once smoked, remove the chipotles from the smoker. To complete the drying process, place them in a dehydrator or an oven set at 200°F and dry them from 6 to 8 hours. When properly dry, the chipotles feel light and sound hollow. Store the fully dried chipotles in an airtight container.

Cooking Techniques

A few simple Mexican cooking techniques need to be addressed as they appear frequently in the recipes in this book: toasting and roasting vegetables, especially chilis, basic sauces, and salsas. To simulate the heating characteristics of a comal, use a flat griddle across two stove burners. These griddles, usually cast from aluminum or iron, are available at kitchen-supply stores.

Toasting Vegetables

The most common vegetables that are toasted in Mexico are onions, garlic, tomatoes, tomatillos, and small green chilis. The handiest and most traditional way to toast them is on a comal. This flat cast-iron griddle is invaluable

for Mexican cooking, inexpensive, and available from many mail-order sources and Mexican markets. (I now keep one on the stove at all times for warming tortillas and toasting bread, nuts, vegetables, and herbs.)

To toast vegetables, heat the comal over fairly high heat and place whole tomatoes, hulled tomatillos, halved and

quartered large onions, small green chilis, or unpeeled garlic on the comal. Turning occasionally (chef's tongs work especially well), cook for 3 to 5 minutes or until the vegetables start to blacken. Once cooked, sweat tomatoes and chilis for a few minutes in a paper or plastic bag for ease of peeling. Peel the toasted vegetables. They are now ready for making into sauce, soup, or salsa. (Rick Bayless, Mexican cooking maven, recommends lining the comal with aluminum foil before roasting tomatoes to avoid the juicy mess and I agree. Diana Kennedy suggests that, if you are roasting large quantities, you broil the tomatoes on a baking sheet a few inches from a hot broiler for 10 to 12 minutes, turning them occasionally.)

If you don't have a comal, use a dry cast-iron frying pan or griddle. Roasting vegetables on an outdoor charcoal barbecue or gas grill works well too, especially for large batches of vegetables. For large chilis and whole small onions, see below.

Roasting Large Chilis

Roasting large chilis calls for a different technique, as the peppers are seldom smooth and the skins need to be evenly charred. You can roast a few large peppers by holding them on a fork in a gas cooktop flame for a few minutes. Turn them constantly to make the skin blacken and blister evenly. If you have an electric stove, put them under the broiler and char them the same way, or char them over a gas grill. If using the broiler of a home oven, brushing the chilis with a little oil helps them to roast more

quickly and evenly. (The goals are to have the chilis roasted but still somewhat firm inside and to make the skins come off readily.) Put the charred peppers in a paper bag to steam for a few minutes for ease of peeling. Scrape the skin off and stem, and seed the chilis. At this point, you can leave them whole for stuffing, cut them into strips, or chop them, depending on the recipe. (If your hands are sensitive, use latex gloves. To prevent burning your eyes, do not rub them while you work with chilis.) Roasted chilis (and tomatoes, too) freeze well in sealable freezer bags.

Chilis con Crema
(Roasted Chili Strips
in Mexican Crema)

Strips of roasted chilis, called *rajas*, with Mexican crema are a traditional way to serve roasted chilis. They make a sublime filling for tacos, quesadillas, and burritos.

    12 fresh green poblanos
    1 1/2 to 2 cups Mexican crema or
        light sour cream
    teaspoon toasted, minced, dried
        Mexican or standard oregano

Roast the chilis according to the preceding directions for roasting large chilis. Cut the roasted chilis into strips. In a double boiler, put the crema or sour cream, roasted chili strips, and oregano; stir to mix. Heat the mixture over simmering water, making sure not to let the water boil, or the crema will curdle. The mixture is ready to serve when it is fairly warm but not simmering.

Serves 4.

Grilled Small Onions
(Cebollitas Asada)

In Mexico, small white immature onions are grilled and served as a sweet, smoky accompaniment to many Mexican meals. Try them chopped, greens and all, with slices of barbecued chicken or beef rolled into a soft, fresh warm tortilla. Serve them with a squirt of lime and salt. Perfection!

Mexicans harvest immature white onions, sometimes called knob onions, less than a few inches across. (See the information on onions in the Encyclopedia.) If you don't have garden onions, these are often available in Mexican grocery stores, or you can substitute large scallions (they take less time to cook).

Mexican-style onions can be cooked over charcoal, on a comal, or—my favorite way—over a gas grill.

    10 to 12 small knob onions
        or 20 scallions
    1 teaspoon vegetable oil

Wash and trim the onions, removing the root end and any scraggly or spoiled leaves. Adjust the gas grill to a fairly low heat. Brush the onions with oil. Place a rectangle of aluminum foil on the grill and drape the onions so that the bulbing parts are directly on the grill and the leaves on the foil. Close the top to the grill. Cook for 8 minutes, using tongs to turn the onions every 2 minutes, until they are golden and tender. It will about 4 minutes more for small onions and 8 for large ones.

Serves 4.

Mexican Cooked Sauces and Salsas

No discussion of Mexican cuisine would be complete without covering salsas and Mexico's special cooking sauces. Sauces of all types are critical to Mexican cuisine, including popular cooked tomato and tomatillo sauces, guacamole, and several types of moles. Sauces in Mexico are seldom thickened with flour or starches; instead, roasted puréed vegetables are used to thicken the sauce, or ground nuts, including almonds, and seeds from pumpkin, sunflower, and sesame are added. Mexican sauces are spicy affairs. Chilis, of course, but also toasted garlic and onions and many spices, including black pepper, cumin, coriander, cloves, and cinnamon, are common. Chocolate is added to some of the famous dark moles. For centuries, most salsas and sauces were made into a paste using a lava rock molcajete, a mortar, and a *tejolote,* a pestle. This process grinds the ingredients and produces a characteristic desirable texture. Few cooks today use these ancient tools; the blender makes it easier to purée sauces and some salsas (not a food processor, as it does an uneven job). Ingredients to be blended must first be chopped or they will blend unevenly and become too soupy by the time the large pieces are done. Blend on low to control the texture. Blender aside, many fresh tomato and tomatillo sauces have the best texture if you chop the ingredients by hand.

Basic Cooked Mexican Tomato Sauce

This basic sauce is great in huevos rancheros, enchiladas, casseroles, and baked chilis rellenos. Like many classic Mexican sauces, it is "fried." The same recipe can be made using about 1 1/2 pounds husked tomatillos instead of the tomatoes.

> 1 medium white onion, quartered
> 2 cloves garlic, unpeeled
> 1 to 2 serranos
> 6 large paste tomatoes
> 1 tablespoon vegetable oil
> 1 teaspoon salt
> 1/2 teaspoon sugar
> 1/2 teaspoon Mexican oregano
> Freshly ground black pepper to taste

First, peel the tomatoes by putting a cross-slit at the base of the tomato and immersing it in boiling water to expand the skin. Then immerse it in ice water to contract the meat away from the skin. Discard the skin. On a hot comal, toast the onion, garlic, serranos, and tomatoes (see page 67). Peel the garlic and remove the seeds from the serranos and the tomatoes. Put all the vegetables into a blender and purée. In a saucepan, heat the vegetable oil. Carefully add the puréed vegetables, which will splatter. Add the salt, sugar, and Mexican oregano; simmer the sauce for about 20 minutes. If the tomatoes are very acidic, add more sugar; if they are sweet, omit the sugar. Season with freshly ground black pepper.

Yields 2 cups.

Mole Verde
(Green Mole with
Vegetables and Seeds)

Moles are an integral part of Mexican cuisine and have numerous variations. Nancy Zaslavsky, author of two invaluable books on Mexican cooking, including *A Cook's Tour of Mexico* and *Meatless Mexican Home Cooking,* contributed this recipe. It was inspired from her work with Juanita Gomez de Hernández in Tehuacán. Nancy recommends serving it over beans, chunks of steamed green vegetables, or rice dishes. I like it in tamales. (For information on toasting vegetables and roasting large chilis, see page 67.)

> 6 poblano chilis
> 1 pound tomatillos

4 jalapeños, stemmed, with seeds
  intact

1 white onion, quartered

4 cloves garlic

2 tablespoons vegetable oil, divided

1/2 pound unsalted, raw shelled
  green pumpkin seeds *(pepitas)*

1/4 cup chopped walnuts or pecans

1/4 cup chopped almonds

2 cups vegetable broth or water

2 teaspoons salt

6 grinds of black pepper

1/2 cup chopped flat-leaf parsley

2 leaves hoja santa, chopped;
  optional

Toast the poblanos. Peel, stem, and remove the seeds and put them in a blender container.

Husk the tomatillos and wash them. Toast the tomatillos and jalapeños on a comal and put them in the blender. Toast the onions and garlic and put them in the blender. Blend the vegetables.

Toast the pumpkin seeds (they will jump around and pop). Put them in the blender. Toast the nuts. Blend them with the pumpkin seeds and 1/2 cup water.

In a large, heavy pot, heat one tablespoon of oil. Add the seed-nut paste and fry it, stirring, for 30 seconds. Turn the heat down to simmer and add the tomatillo mixture, adding more oil, if necessary. Add the broth, salt, and pepper. Cook until all the broth is incorporated and the sauce is slightly thickened, about 20 minutes. Blend the parsley and the hoja santa with enough water to purée and add. Taste carefully and adjust the seasonings.

Serves 6.

Guacamole

Guacamole is a fabulous dish made of puréed avocados. It often accompanies tacos, huevos rancheros, and tortas. I have strong opinions about guacamole. I feel it should always be made with rich buttery avocados, not those watery kinds sometimes available in the market, and it should glorify the taste of the avocado, not be watered down with sour cream and such. Guacamole is best made just before serving, as it turns brown rather quickly.

1 large 'Hass,' 'Bacon,' or other
  rich avocado

1 teaspoon lime juice

1–2 teaspoons chopped fresh
  cilantro

pinch of salt

Optional: 1/4 cup fresh salsa and 2
  dried Mexican-type avocado
  leaves, 3 inches long, finely
  ground

Peel the avocado, remove the seed, and mash the flesh. Add the lime juice, cilantro, salt, and optional salsa and avocado leaves, if using. Stir the mixture well and put it in a serving bowl.

Makes about 1/2 cup.

Salsas

Salsas are ubiquitous in Mexico and the fastest-growing segment of the North American condiment market as well. Chilis, both fresh or dried, are the common denominator in salsas and the infinite variations range widely in flavor and spiciness, depending on the technique and ingredients used. While the most common salsas are tomato based, in Mexico, one also enjoys salsas of different roasted, fresh chopped chilis mixed with a little lime juice, green salsas made from either cactus paddles or cucumbers, tomatillo-based salsas, and even one made with ground pumpkin seeds and crema.

Cooked salsas are delicious and have the advantage of keeping longer when refrigerated or frozen. Raw or cooked salsas may be canned. Use a recipe designed for canning, as vinegar may have to be added for acidity to prevent botulism. The following salsas give a great range of flavors and will become staples on your Mexican table.

Salsa Fresca (Fresh Salsa)

Here is a classic tomato salsa to serve with tacos, huevos rancheros, pozole, and tortas. It is best used promptly, but leftover sauce can be refrigerated to keep about 5 days.

2 to 4 fresh serranos or jalapeños

1/2 medium white onion, minced

2 cloves garlic, pressed or minced

4 large, ripe tomatoes, minced and
  seeded

3 tablespoons fresh minced cilantro

Salt to taste

Stem the chilis (seed, too, if you desire a milder salsa) and then mince. Combine them with the remaining ingredients and serve in a small bowl so diners can serve themselves.

Makes 3 cups.

should be a little runnier than apple-sauce, so add water if needed.

Makes approximately 1/3 cup.

Greens, Mexican Style

Most greens are all cooked in similar fashion. Called *quelites* in Mexico, some greens are wild and gathered from the fields; others are cultivated. Among the most popular in Mexico are the leaf amaranths, purslane, Swiss chard, spinach, and huauzontlí.

    10 cups greens
    1 tablespoon vegetable oil
    1 white onion, minced
    1 serrano, minced
    1 clove garlic, minced
    3 medium tomatoes, peeled and
        chopped
    Garnish: 2 tablespoons crumbled,
        aged Mexican cheese

Wash the greens and remove tough stems. Put the greens in a pot, cover, and steam for 5 minutes. Do not add water. Remove the greens from the pot, cool, and set aside. Heat the oil in the pot and sauté the onion, serrano, and garlic until they are soft. Chop the greens, and add the tomatoes and the greens to the pot. Mix and cook them for 5 minutes. Garnish with the crumbled cheese.

Serves 4.

Salsa Verde (Tomatillo Salsa)

This traditional green salsa is made from tomatillos. Try it with roasted or barbecued pork, scrambled eggs, tamales, burritos, and in tacos. It keeps for about 5 days in the refrigerator.

    20 large tomatillos about 1 1/2
        inches in diameter
    1 tablespoon oil
    2 or 3 fresh serranos or jalapeños,
        minced
    1 medium white onion, minced
    2 cloves garlic, minced
    1/4 teaspoon sugar
    Salt to taste
    2 tablespoons minced fresh cilantro

Husk the tomatillos and wash them. Put them in a saucepan, add 1/2 cup water, and simmer them, covered, until just tender, about 5 minutes. Drain, cool, and mince.

Heat the oil in a nonstick sauté pan and add the tomatillos, chilis, onions, garlic, and sugar. Cook the vegetables over medium heat, stirring, for about 5 minutes. Add the salt. Cool, stir in the cilantro, and serve.

Makes 2 1/2 cups.

Salsa Cruda

This is the smoky, intense salsa Doug Kaufmann, chef and chili maven, gave me. It uses mulato chilis, but anchos are great too. This traditional Mexican salsa is enjoyed on warm corn or flour tortillas, as an appetizer or to accompany an entrée.

    2 mulato chilis
    2 cloves garlic, peeled

Cut the chilis in two; deseed and devein for a mild salsa. In a dry cast-iron skillet or comal, toast the chilis over medium heat; turn them often to avoid burning them. When they get aromatic, in about 1 minute, take them off the heat and put them in a small bowl. Cover the chilis with hot water and let them sit for 20 to 30 minutes. Remove them from the water and place them in a blender or a food processor. (Use a traditional *molcajete* if you have one.) Add the garlic and 1/4 cup of the soaking water and blend for 1 minute on low speed. Scrape the mixture down and blend until the chilis are ground. The consistency

Other Ingredients to Have on Hand

Armed with this book, you can grow a majority of the vegetables and herbs most popular in Mexico. Here are explanations of a few more ingredients common in Mexican cooking.

Avocados (aguacate): Numerous types of avocados are on the market, primarily of either Guatemalan or Mexican descent. Some are quite watery and not suitable for Mexican dishes. Look for 'Hass' and 'Bacon' and, in the winter, the 'Fuerte,' as they have a high oil content and rich flavor.

Purchase avocados when they are hard or when they have just started to soften. They are ready when they give when pressed and the flesh is firm but buttery.

Occasionally, in southern Mexico, crumbled, dried avocado leaves are used in tamales and sprinkled over refried beans. The leaves of the Mexican avocado taste of anise and nuts; the Guatemalan avocado leaves have no flavor.

Cheeses (queso): The three most important cheeses used in Mexican cooking are queso fresca, a soft, mild melting cheese—if not available, substitute with mozzarella or Monterey Jack; queso anejo (including *cotija*), an aged, crumbly, strong-flavored cheese—substitute with a mild feta; and the creamy, rich crema Mexicana that is similar to crème fraîche and sour cream.

Cooking fats and oils: The primary fats of Mexico are vegetable oils and lard. A number of vegetable oils are used, including corn and safflower, which are great for frying tortillas and some vegetables. While folks are skittish about using lard, in fact, home-rendered lard *(manteca)* has 20 percent less saturated fat than butter and lots of delicious roasted pork flavor. Just as I occasionally use butter as a treat, I also use my homemade lard, as it makes a huge difference in the flavor of dishes like tortilla soup (see recipe, page 76). To render your own lard, purchase a pound or so of pork fat and cut in small cubes. Put it in a deep ovenproof dish and bake at 325°F for 1 1/2 to 2 1/2 hours or until most of the fat is rendered and the pork starts to brown. As it cooks, pour the fat off into a sterilized pint jar. Strain the remaining fat, cover the jar, and refrigerate the lard. The crispy pork pieces can be used for garnishing refried beans, added to tacos, or fed to birds. The lard will harden some and remain fresh tasting for a month or so.

Limes: North of the border, lemons are the citrus of choice; in Mexico, limes *(limones)* are favored. Both the familiar large limes and the sour, small Mexican limes (also known as Key limes) are added to many sauces, including guacamole, salsas, fruit drinks, onion marinade, and seafood. Key lime is available in large Mexican grocery stores and in many supermarkets in Florida.

Fruit Salad with Jícama
(Ensalada de Fruita)

With so many tropical fruits available in Mexico, salads with many types of fruits, dusted with chili powder, are common. Often jícama, cucumbers, or fresh coconut slices are included. According to Luis Torres, this is a common potluck dish north of the border as well. The salad can be made with just about any combination of tropical fruits and offered without the chili and accompanied by a shaker of chili powder, allowing diners to season the fruit themselves. Serve the salad either room temperature or chilled.

1 small jícama (about ³/₄ pound) peeled and cubed

1 small papaya (about ¹/₂ pound)

1 mango

2 cups of watermelon cubes

2 cups of cantaloupe cubes

Juice of 1 large lime

1–3 teaspoons powdered California chilis for a mild salad, 'Chili de Arbol' for a spicy one

Combine the jícama and fruits in a bowl and sprinkle them with the lime juice and chili powder. Serve room temperature or chilled.

Serves 6 to 8.

Cactus Paddle Salad

(Ensalada de Nopalitos)

Luis Torres showed me how to make this wonderful salad after we made a visit to the Mercado in Los Angeles. We served it with tortillas, refried beans, carne asada (roasted beef), and salsa. He says he also serves it with tacos and burritos, as a salad side dish, and takes it to barbecues and potlucks. See the prickly pear entry in the Encyclopedia for information on preparing the cactus paddles.

Approximately 6 young cactus paddles *(nopales)*, spines removed, cut in ³/₄-inch squares (approximately 4 cups)

¹/₂ teaspoon salt

2 cloves garlic, minced

3–4 large paste tomatoes cut in ¹/₄-inch dice (2 cups)

¹/₄ cup chopped fresh cilantro

¹/₃ cup chopped white onion

3 ounces queso fresca or aged Mexican cheese

Juice of ¹/₂ lime

In a large saucepan, bring 6 cups of water to a boil. Add the salt, garlic, and cactus paddles; simmer over medium heat until the paddles are tender (This could take anywhere from 15–45 minutes, depending on desired consistency). Drain them in a colander. Rinse the cooked paddles for 5 minutes or so under hot running water, swishing them around to remove some of the slippery juice.

In a medium bowl, put the cactus paddles, tomatoes, cilantro, onions, and cheese. Squeeze the lime over the ingredients and gently stir. Adjust the seasonings, as different brands of cheese have different amounts of salt. Put the mixture in the refrigerator to chill.

Serves 4 to 6.

Cool White Salad

This recipe was created especially for me by Carole Saville, who designs culinary gardens for restaurants and writes herb books. While not traditional, it captures the spirit of Mexico.

2 tablespoons lime juice

1/4 teaspoon cumin

Salt to taste

Freshly ground white pepper to
    taste

Pinch cayenne pepper

6 tablespoons corn oil

1 tablespoons cilantro, chopped
    fine

1 large or 2 small jícamas

Garnish: slices of sweet white
    onion; sliced orange halves

In a mixing bowl, combine lime juice, cumin, salt, white pepper, and cayenne pepper. Slowly whisk in the oil until dressing is emulsified. Add cilantro and mix again. Peel jícama and cut into thin matchsticks. Pour dressing over jícama and mix well. Garnish with onions and orange. Chill salad in the refrigerator.

Serves 6.

Tortilla Soup

(Sopa Azteca)

This rich and surprising soup is one of my favorite dishes. Its many flavors contrasting with the crisp tortillas and creamy avocados give your mouth a lot to think about. Serve it as a first course as is, or add beans and chicken meat for a filling entrée. As with many Mexican dishes, the garnishes are integral and allow diners to season the dish as they please. See page 67 for more information on toasting vegetables.

For the broth:

    4 cloves garlic, unpeeled
    1 white onion, peeled
    6 large paste tomatoes
    8 cups chicken stock
    2 tablespoons lard or vegetable oil
    3–4 fresh epazote leaves, chopped;
        or 1 teaspoon dried oregano
    Salt and freshly ground black
        pepper to taste

To make the broth: Heat a dry comal until very hot. Toast the garlic cloves in their skins until golden. Cut the onion into 8 sections and toast them in the same manner. Toast the tomatoes until their skins blister. Peel and seed the tomatoes. Peel the garlic. In a blender, purée the toasted garlic, onions, tomatoes and 1/4 cup of the chicken stock. This can be done in two batches.

In a large soup pot, heat the lard. Carefully, because it splatters, add the purée. Reduce the heat and cook, stirring, about 10 to 15 minutes until the purée gets thick and darkens in color.

Pour in the remaining chicken stock and the epazote or oregano; simmer for about 20 minutes. Season with salt and pepper to taste.

For the garnish:

    2 chipotles
    2 dried anchos
    2 cups vegetable oil, divided
    6–8 stale corn tortillas
    1 large ripe avocado
    1/2 pound queso fresco
    1/4 cup + 1 tablespoon crema or
        sour cream
    1/2 cup chopped cilantro
    3 limes, quartered

Remove the stems and seeds from the chilis and cut them into strips 1/8 inch wide. In a frying pan, heat 1 tablespoon of the vegetable oil and fry the chilis, stirring, for 30 seconds. Drain them on a paper towel and set them aside. Stack the corn tortillas; cut them

into quarters and then into strips $1/4$ inch wide. Add the remaining oil to the frying pan; heat the oil and fry the tortilla strips until they are golden. Remove them from the oil with a slotted spoon and drain them on a paper towel; set aside. Cut the avocado and the queso fresco into 1-inch cubes.

To serve the soup: Reheat the broth and ladle individual servings into 4 shallow bowls. Add a few avocado and cheese cubes, sprinkle with fried chilis, and top with tortilla strips. Add a tablespoon of crema, sprinkle with cilantro, and serve with lime wedges. Pass separate bowls of the garnishes so diners can add more if they want to fine-tune their dish.

Serves 4.

Malva and Zucchini Soup

(Sopa de Alache y Calabacitas)

This lovely, light soup was given to me by Ed Walsh and Tess McDonough, the chefs at Kendall Jackson Winery. They try many authentic recipes from Mexico, including this one, made with *alache,* a kind of malva that grows wild in much of the West (see the wild greens entry in the Encyclopedia). Ed says this type of soup is considered to aid digestion in Mexico and is often served before a rich meal of pork or a mole. He suggests that any other vegetable that lends thickening to the soup—chopped nopales blanched for 5 minutes, sliced okra, or chopped purslane—would work in place of the alache. Further, he says the soup is even better if you make it the day before, as the flavors meld and the alache thickens to soup.

1 cup alache leaves

2 tablespoons vegetable oil

1 small white onion, chopped

3 cloves garlic, peeled and diced

1 cup green summer squash cut in
 medium dice

Salt and pepper to taste

To blanche alache leaves, drop them into boiling salted water for 5 to 10 seconds or until they wilt. Drain them in a colander.

Put the oil in a medium pot, heat over medium heat, add the onion and garlic, and sauté until the onion is translucent. Add 3 cups of water (or substitute chicken stock for a more flavorful sopa), the alache, and the squash. Add salt and pepper to taste. Simmer on low for about 40 minutes or until the squash breaks down. Serve warm with tortillas.

Serves 4.

in the stock and simmer until the squash breaks down and the soup is creamy. Remove it from the heat and stir in the poblano and the sugar. Serve in heated bowls.

To serve the soup in a pumpkin or squash, first cut the top out of a pumpkin as you would a jack-o'-lantern. Clean out the pumpkin with a sharp spoon. Make a few tablespoons of the herbal butter using the preceding proportions and method. Brush the insides and the rim of the cleaned-out pumpkin with the butter. To provide a bit of a smoky flavor, hold the pumpkin upside down over a charcoal fire or grill for a few minutes. Pour the squash soup into the pumpkin. To match the photo, sprinkle a little coarse salt around the rim as if it were a margarita glass.

Serves 4 to 6.

Winter Squash Soup

(Sopa de Calabaza)

This soup, like the preceding one, is from Ed Walsh and Tess McDonough, and has great Mexican flavors. For a dramatic presentation, Ed likes to serve the soup in a pumpkin or winter squash. This rich soup makes a terrific first course.

> 2 tablespoons butter
> 1 teaspoon fresh sage, chopped
> 1 teaspoon fresh marjoram, chopped
> 1 teaspoon fresh oregano, chopped
> 4 cups peeled and diced banana or butternut squash
> 1/4 teaspoon cinnamon
> 1/4 teaspoon ground cloves
> Salt and freshly ground black pepper to taste
> 3 cups chicken stock
> 1 poblano, roasted, peeled, and diced
> 1 teaspoon sugar
> Salt to taste (if using unsalted stock)
> Garnish: coarse salt, 1 tablespoon Mexican crema or sour cream

In a large saucepot, melt the butter and add the sage, marjoram, and oregano. Allow to cook over low heat until the butter starts to brown but not burn, approximately 5 minutes. Once the butter is golden brown, remove the pot from the heat, strain the butter, and discard the herbs. Place the strained butter back in the pot and sauté the squash, cinnamon, cloves, salt, and pepper for approximately 10 minutes, until the squash starts to soften. Pour

Red Pozole

(Pozole Rojo)

Pozole is a Mexican classic soup most often eaten in restaurants. As with any popular dish, recipes differ from region to region and from cook to cook, but all include pozole corn and chilis in some form. There are two basic types: a green one made with tomatillos, fresh chilis, pumpkin seeds, and herbs; and the following red one, made with dried chilis and tomatoes.

This pozole can be made with your own home-grown and hominied dent corn (see page 65), or you can buy frozen or canned pozole corn. (I much prefer the frozen form.) The many garnishes are a traditional part of the dish.

For the stock:

2 tablespoons vegetable oil

1 chicken, cut into serving pieces

1 medium white onion, finely
    chopped

2 quarts chicken broth

4 whole cloves

2 bay leaves

To make the stock: In a large soup pot, heat the oil and brown the chicken pieces. Add the onion and cook until golden. Add the chicken broth, cloves, and bay leaves. (These can be tied in a small piece of cheesecloth and removed after the cooking is done.) Simmer the chicken for 20 minutes. Remove the chicken pieces. Set the chicken and the stock aside.

For the soup base:

3 dried pasilla chilis

3 dried guajillo chilis

3 large tomatoes, seeded

6 cloves garlic, unpeeled

1 medium white onion, peeled and
    quartered

To make the soup base: Open the chilis and remove the seeds and membranes. On a hot comal, toast the chilis until they perfume the air, about 30 seconds. Put them in a bowl, cover with hot water, and let them soak for 30 minutes. Toast the tomatoes, garlic, and

onion on a comal or grill. (See the information on toasting vegetables on page 67.) Put the roasted tomatoes, garlic, onion, and chilis, plus 1/4 cup of the chili soaking water, into a blender; puree the vegetables into a smooth paste. Set aside.

To finish the soup:

2 tablespoons vegetable oil

6 cups pozole corn

1 tablespoon dried Mexican
    oregano

Salt and fresh black pepper to taste

Garnish:

1 chopped avocado

1 chopped tomato

1 small white onion, chopped

1/2 cup chopped cilantro

Lime wedges

In a large soup pot, heat the oil. Add the soup base purée (carefully, as it splatters) and fry over medium heat for

3 minutes. Add the chicken stock and bring to a boil. Add the pozole corn and cook for 3 to 4 hours or until tender (if you use frozen pozole corn, it takes about 30 minutes; canned pozole takes even less). To serve, add the chicken pieces back to the soup. Fill individual shallow bowls with the pozole. Put the garnishes in small bowls so diners can garnish their own plate.

Serves 4 to 6.

Chayote Sauté with Chilis

1 1/2 pounds chayote (about 3 large)

2 teaspoons vegetable oil

2 cloves garlic, thinly sliced

Minced chilis to taste: 1/2 tablespoon jalapeño for mild, 1/2 tablespoon serrano for medium, or 1 teaspoon, or more, habañero for blazing

1/2 teaspoon crumbled dried Mexican oregano leaves

1/4 teaspoon salt

2 tablespoons water

Garnish: 1 tablespoon fresh chopped cilantro

Chayotes are delicate-tasting, slightly sweet squashlike vegetables. They can be simply sautéed in a little oil and enjoyed as is or sauced with tomatoes and sprinkled with cheese or minced chilis of any measure of hotness to create a spicy side dish like the following. Serve this dish to accompany egg, cheese, fish, and chicken dishes or add it to tacos or burritos.

Peel chayote and cut it into slices 1/4 inch thick, including the seed, which is edible. Pour oil into a medium sauté pan, heat over fairly low heat, and add the chayote. Sauté for about 10 minutes or until the chayote starts to brown slightly, stirring occasionally so it cooks evenly and doesn't get too brown. Add the garlic and sauté lightly. Add the chilis, oregano, salt, and water, stir, and cover; simmer until the squash is tender and translucent, about 5 minutes. Transfer to a warm serving dish and garnish with cilantro.

Serves 4.

Fava Beans with Tomatoes

(Habas y Jitomates)

Fava beans are enjoyed in Mexico and this is one of the most popular ways to serve them. The same recipes can be used for snap beans as well. Just add cooked beans to the sauce and simmer for 2 or 3 minutes.

4–5 pounds fresh fava beans, shelled (about 4 cups)

To prepare the beans: Remove the fava beans from their pods. Boil them in water for 5 minutes. Drain and cool. Remove the tough skins by cutting a small slit at one end of the bean and, with your index finger and thumb, squeezing the bean from its skin.

For the sauce:

1 white onion

2 cloves garlic, unpeeled

4 paste tomatoes

1 teaspoon lard

1/2 teaspoon dried Mexican oregano

1 teaspoon salt

To make the sauce: Peel the onion and cut it into 8 wedges. Heat a comal or cast-iron pan and toast the onion wedges until golden brown and the unpeeled garlic until soft, about 10 minutes. Cool and peel the garlic. Toast the tomatoes until their skins start to blister. Cool them, peel, and remove the seeds. Place the toasted onion, garlic, and tomatoes into a blender and purée until smooth. In a saucepan, heat the lard and fry the tomato purée—be careful, it splatters—for about 3 minutes. Add 1 1/2 cups water, Mexican oregano, and salt.

Add the fava beans (or cooked snap beans) to the sauce; simmer for 5 to 10 minutes or until the beans are soft but don't fall apart.

Serves 4.

Esquites

Kit Anderson bought this snacklike dish from a street vendor in Chapingo, Mexico, when she was visiting Professor Garrison Wilkes, a geneticist specializing in preserving corn varieties. She liked it so much we asked Professor Wilkes to track down the recipe. Esquites can be made with either field corn picked at the milk stage or with fresh, ripe sweet corn. In some versions, the corn is not fried in oil first, as it is here. Vendors sell it in cups with a spoon.

    3/4 cup oil or lard

    1 medium onion, chopped

    4 1/2 pounds corn kernels cut off
        the cobs

    optional: 1/2 pound longaniza
        sausage (found in Asian mar-
        kets; substitute linguica.)

    2–5 serrano chilies, finely chopped,
        to taste

    8 tomatillos, quartered

    Half a handful epazote, chopped

    1–2 tablespoons salt

Heat oil or lard in a large, heavy pot and sauté the onion. Add the corn, sausage, and chilis and fry over medium heat, stirring occasionally, until corn is slightly browned. Add the remaining ingredients and enough water to moisten slightly, cover, and simmer until corn is tender, 10 to 15 minutes.

Makes enough for a fiesta.

Huevos Rancheros

This is my favorite breakfast. I find it works best to make the tomato sauce and refried beans the day before. Not only do they taste better but when I'm still sleepy, all I have to do is assemble the dish.

    2 cups basic tomato sauce (see
        recipe, page 69)

    5 cups refried beans (see recipe,
        page 63)

    1–2 tablespoons vegetable oil

    8 corn tortillas

    8 eggs

    Salt and freshly ground black
        pepper to taste

Garnish:

    1/4 cup crumbled queso fresca

    1/4 cup chopped cilantro

Bring the tomato sauce and the refried beans to serving temperature and keep warm. Warm your serving plates. In a nonstick frying pan over medium heat, heat the oil and cook the tortillas, one at a time, for about 30 seconds each or until the tortilla starts to puff up and soften. Drain the tortillas on a paper towel and keep them in a warm oven. Fry the eggs in the remaining oil. To serve, put two tortillas on a plate; spread them with a generous amount of tomato sauce. Place the fried eggs on top of the tomato sauce. Serve about 3/4 cups refried beans for each diner. Sprinkle the eggs with salt, pepper, and cilantro. Garnish the beans with the crumbled queso fresca.

Serves 4.

Quesadillas

Traditional quesadillas are corn tortillas or masa folded over a cheese filling and fried. Sometimes chopped and cooked nopales or squash blossoms are added. In the Southwest, the concept has expanded, and some families (like mine) eat quesadillas day and night as either a snack or light meal and make them with both the traditional corn tortillas and flour tortillas. I find it easier to cook a sandwich quesadilla, with a bottom and a top tortilla, than the traditional folded-in-half tortilla. It's easier to manage on the comal and I can use less-than-fresh tortillas because stale ones crack when folded.

4 corn tortillas
$1/2$–$2/3$ cup crumbled queso fresca or grated plain or hot pepper Monterey Jack cheese
$1/2$ cup julienned roasted poblanos
Cilantro

Heat a comal, well-seasoned cast-iron skillet, or nonstick sauté pan over fairly high heat. Place two tortillas on a clean, dry surface. Sprinkle half of the cheese, half of the chili strips, and a few leaves of cilantro on each tortilla. Cover each with another tortilla. Put 1 filled tortilla sandwich on the comal. Press down occasionally with a spatula. When the cheese melts, you can turn the tortilla sandwich over without it coming apart; turn and cook the other side until it starts to get slightly golden in spots. Turn it back over and cook until the first side is slightly golden as well. Transfer the quesadilla to a warm serving plate and repeat the process with the second quesadilla. Cut each quesadilla into 4 pie-shaped wedges. Serve with salsa and/or guacamole in which to dip the quesadillas.

Serves 1 for lunch.

Bean Burritos

Burritos are popular in parts of northern Mexico and even more popular north of the border, especially at our house. Burritos are like rolled sandwiches and exist in infinite variations. You can add leftover chicken, beef, pork, or scrambled eggs, chopped tomatoes, even grated cabbage. The amounts given in this recipe are but a starting point—you'll probably never make them the same way twice. Use only fresh flour tortillas; don't let them dry out in the oven or the tortillas will crack when you try to roll them into a burrito.

1 1/2–2 cups refried beans
1/2–3/4 cup roasted, peeled
    poblanos cut in narrow strips or
    one 4-ounce can whole green
    chilis
4 burrito-size flour tortillas
1/2–3/4 cup fresh salsa
4 tablespoons guacamole
4 tablespoon sour cream
1/2 cup grated jalapeño Monterey
    Jack cheese
Cilantro

Heat the refried beans. In a separate pan, heat the chilis. Keep both warm. Heat the flour tortillas on a lightly greased nonstick frying pan or comal until warm and just starting to brown. Turn each one 2 or 3 times to keep them heating evenly. To keep them warm, place them, covered with a slightly damp tea towel, in a warm oven (200°F) until you are ready to assemble the burritos.

To assemble, place one flour tortilla on a clean work surface. Place a quarter of the beans in the center of the lower half of the tortilla. Place a quarter of the chilis on top of the beans. Sprinkle a few tablespoons each of salsa and cheese and 1 tablespoon each of guacamole and sour cream over the chilis. Add a few sprigs of cilantro, if you like. Fold the bottom up and the sides in, then roll to form a burrito.

Serves 4.

Tortilla Casserole

Casseroles are a fairly modern dish in Mexico, as few cooks had ovens before the 1940s. This rich casserole is a great way to use stale corn tortillas. It can be made with either zucchini or chayote. My daughter-in-law, Julie Creasy, a Mexican food lover, helped me develop this recipe. Assembling the casserole is a bit like layering a lasagna. Serve with a green salad.

Vegetable oil, as needed

4 zucchinis, 4 inches round or long, sliced lengthwise (or 3 medium chayote, sliced, and 1 serrano chili)

16–20 stale corn tortillas

4–5 cups basic cooked tomato sauce (see page 69)

2 cups Monterey Jack cheese, grated, divided

2 ears corn, boiled, kernels removed from the cob

2/3 cup Mexican crema or sour cream

1/2 teaspoon dried Mexican or standard oregano

1/2 cup roasted poblanos, chopped

1/2 cup anejo cheese or mild feta, crumbled

Brush the zucchini with oil and grill them over medium heat on a charcoal or gas grill until they are tender but not too soft. Alternately, sauté the zucchini or chayote with the serrano chili in 1 teaspoon of oil in a nonstick frying pan until soft. Set aside.

Grease a 9-by-13-inch ovenproof baking dish. Briefly sauté the tortillas, one at a time, in a nonstick frying pan, using 1 teaspoon or so of oil for every 3 or 4 tortillas. (The tortillas need a light coating of oil to prevent them from becoming too soggy in the sauce.) Transfer the tortillas to the bottom of the baking pan as they become supple and heated through. Create a single layer of tortillas; pour 2 cups of sauce over it and spread evenly to cover. Arrange the cooked zucchini or chayote in an even layer over the sauce. Sprinkle 1 cup grated Jack cheese and the corn kernels over the squash. Create another layer of tortillas and spread it with the crema. Sprinkle the poblanos and oregano over the crema.

Make a final layer of softened tortillas on top and spread the remaining sauce over them. Sprinkle 1 cup Jack cheese over the sauce and top with the crumbled anejo or feta cheese. Bake at 350°F for 30 to 35 minutes or until the casserole is bubbling and the Jack cheese is melted. Let cool for a few minutes before serving.

Serves 4 to 6.

Pork Shoulder Sandwiches with Tomatillos
(Tortas de Piernas)

These sandwiches are variations on ones shown to me by Luis Torres and his sister Virginia Vasquez. Virginia's brother-in-law, Javier Vasquez, who sold similar tortas from his *puesto* (food stand) in Guadalajara, was the original inspiration. Virginia and Luis now make them for parties in Los Angeles. The best way to describe these sandwiches is as sloppy joes with a south-of-the-border flavor.

For the meat filling:

5 pounds fresh pork shoulder

5–8 dried bay leaves (or 8 fresh bay leaves)

1/2 tablespoon whole cloves

1 1/2 tablespoons vegetable oil

1 large white onion, chopped finely

4 cups finely chopped tomatillos

2 large tomatoes, chopped finely

7-ounce can chipotle en adobo (the amount you use depends on how much heat you want)

1 teaspoon cumin seeds

1/4 teaspoon ground cloves

Salt to taste

To prepare the meat filling: Cut the pork off the bones into pieces approximately 2 by 3 inches. Remove large pieces of fat but retain the bones. In a 12-quart kettle, put 2 quarts of water and bring to a boil. Tie the bay leaves and cloves in cheesecloth. Put the pork, the bones, and the cheesecloth bag into the boiling water. Simmer the pork for 2 hours, uncovered for the first hour, covered for the second hour, until it is very tender and shreds readily.

In the meantime, over medium heat, in a large frying pan, heat the oil; add the onions and sauté them for about 6 minutes or until they are translucent and just starting to brown. Add the tomatillos and sauté for about 5 minutes, then add the tomatoes and simmer for 10 minutes or until they are tender.

Heat a dry skillet and toast the cumin seeds for a minute or so until they start to perfume the air. Grind the seeds in a spice grinder or mortar and pestle. In a blender, put the chipotle en adobo, the ground cumin, and the ground cloves. Add 1/2 cup of the pork cooking liquid and blend until smooth. Add the chipotle mixture to the tomatillo mixture and cook over

medium heat, stirring, for about 5 minutes.

When the pork is tender, drain it into a colander, saving the broth (you should have between 2 and 3 cups of broth). If you like your sandwiches especially sloppy, keep the 3 cups; if you prefer them a little drier, boil the liquid down to 2 cups.

Remove the bag of spices and the bones and discard them. Put the meat into a large bowl and cool. With your fingers, pull the meat into shreds; this can also be done with a potato masher. Return the reserved broth to the pot. Add the meat and the tomatillo mixture to the broth and bring it back to a simmer. Once hot, prepare the sandwiches or refrigerate and reheat to serve the next day.

For the sandwich:

8–12 bolillo (Mexican rolls) or 6-inch French sandwich rolls

8 tablespoons butter (1 stick)
6 medium tomatoes, sliced
1 head iceberg lettuce, thinly sliced
1 large white onion, thinly sliced
Juice of 1/2 lime
1 cup crema or sour cream

Put the onion slices in a small bowl and marinate them in the lime juice for 20 minutes. Cut the rolls lengthwise until nearly halved. Liberally butter the rolls and toast them on a medium to hot comal or grill until they are quite brown. Make them into sandwiches with dollops of warm pork mixture, sliced onion, tomato, lettuce, and crema to taste. Add mariachi music and enjoy!

Serves 8 to 10.

Pork Stew with Purslane

This is a classic Mexican recipe. Nopales or chard can be used instead of the purslane and pork short ribs for the pork loin. Serve the stew with corn tortillas and, for garnishing; fresh salsa, chopped cilantro, and crema, if you choose. Leftover stew is great the next day served with warm tortillas.

For the sauce base:

> 1 pound tomatillos, husked
>
> 2–4 serranos
>
> 1 small white onion, quartered
>
> 2 cloves garlic, unpeeled
>
> 1/2 cup beef broth
>
> 1/2 cup cilantro, chopped
>
> Salt to taste

To make the sauce base: On a hot comal, toast the tomatillos, serranos, onions, and garlic until brown. Remove the seeds from the serranos and the skin from the garlic. In a blender, purée the toasted vegetables with the beef broth until smooth. Add the chopped cilantro and salt, stir, and set aside.

For the stew:

> 2 tablespoons vegetable oil
>
> 1 1/2 pounds pork loin, cut into 1-inch cubes
>
> 1 medium white onion, finely chopped
>
> 1 clove garlic, minced
>
> 6 Yukon gold or red boiling pota-

toes, peeled and quartered

> 3 cups purslane shoots, thick stems removed (usually grows wild in cultivated fields, and is more likely found at a farm stand than at the supermarket)
>
> 1 teaspoon dried Mexican oregano
>
> Salt to taste
>
> Garnish: chopped cilantro

To make the stew: Preheat the oven to 325°F. In a heavy-bottomed, ovenproof pot with a cover, or a Dutch oven, heat the oil. Add the pork and brown over medium heat, about 15 to 20 minutes. (You probably need to do this in at least 2 batches.) Remove the meat from the pot and set aside. Sauté the onions and garlic in the same pot over low heat until tender. Add the tomatillo sauce base and bring it to a rolling boil; add the meat, cover the pot, and bake in the oven for 30 minutes. Add the potatoes, cover, and bake for 20–30 more min-

utes or until the potatoes are tender. Add the purslane and cook 5 minutes more. On a hot comal or dry frying pan, toast the Mexican oregano for about 30 seconds; cool and crumble. Season the stew with the oregano and salt. Serve with the chopped cilantro.

Serves 4.

Melon Cooler

(Agua de Sandia)

In a hot climate such as Mexico's, cool, refreshing fruit drinks are a must—a part of everyday life. Often such Mexican drinks include melons, either watermelon or cantaloupe, from the garden. This version includes tequila but rum could be used, or it could be made without any alcohol at all—it would be equally delicious. The following proportions I find pleasing and not too sweet, but you may want to add more sugar or lime juice. I make it light on the tequila so I can enjoy more than one glass.

1/2 small watermelon, large seeds
removed, cubed
1–2 tablespoons sugar
Juice of 1 1/2 limes
2 shots tequila
Garnish: spearmint leaves

Put the watermelon cubes in a blender or food processor bowl, add 1 cup of water; and blend until fairly smooth. (You may have to do this in more than one batch.) Strain the juice to remove the seeds. (This is usually necessary even with seedless watermelons, as they have small white vestigial seeds.) Add the sugar and lime juice, stir, and adjust the flavorings to suit your taste. The mixture can be refrigerated for a few hours at this point.

Before serving, add the tequila and stir. Chill 4 large glasses, then fill them half full of shaved ice. Pour the watermelon mixture over the ice and garnish each glass with mint leaves.

Makes about 1 quart.

Jamaica Tea

(Agua Jamaica)

This tea has a slight cranberry flavor and will be familiar to people who have had Red Zinger tea, of which jamaica is an integral part.

    4 cups of water
    1/2 cup dried jamaica calyxes
    1/4–1/2 cups sugar
    Garnish: orange slices

In a medium saucepan, bring the water to a boil. Add the jamaica, turn off the heat, and let the mixture steep for 5 minutes. If a stronger flavor is desired, use more tea leaves. Add the sugar and adjust the sweetness. Serve hot as is or let it cool slightly and pour over shaved ice. Garnish each cup or glass with a slice of orange.

Serves 4.

Iceberg Cooler

Olivia Montanez of the Imperial Spice Company remembers her father making a cooling drink by thinly slicing half a head of iceberg lettuce, soaking it in limes, sugar, and water for a few hours, and pouring it over ice.

appendix A planting and maintenance

Covered in this section are the basics of planning a vegetable garden, preparing the soil, starting seeds, transplanting, fertilizing, mulching, composting, installing irrigation and watering, weeding, crop rotation, and using floating row covers.

Planning Your Vegetable Garden

You can interplant Mexican vegetables and herbs among your ornamental flowers—many, such as amaranth and peppers, are quite beautiful—raise them in large containers or planter boxes, or add them to your existing vegetable garden. If you have no vegetable garden, you can design one. The first step in planning any vegetable garden is choosing a suitable site. Most chefs recommend locating the edible garden as close to the kitchen as possible, and I heartily agree. Beyond that, the majority of vegetables need at least six hours of sun (eight is better)—except in warm, humid areas, where afternoon or some filtered shade is best. Most annual vegetables also need fairly rich, well-drained soil with lots of added organic matter.

Take note of what type of soil you have and how well it drains. Annual vegetables need to grow fast and with little stress to be tender and mild. Their roots need air and, if the soil stays waterlogged for long, roots suffocate or are prone to root rot. If you are unsure how well a particular area in your garden drains, dig a hole about 10 inches deep and 10 inches across and fill it with water. The next day, fill it again; if it still has water in it eight to ten hours later, you need to find another place in the garden that will drain much faster. Amend your soil with much organic matter and mound it up at least 6 to 8 inches above the ground level, or grow your vegetables in containers. A very sandy soil that drains too fast also calls for the addition of copious amounts of organic matter.

Find out, too, what your soil pH is. Nurseries have kits to test your soil's pH and University Extension Services can lead you to sources of soil tests and soil experts. Most vegetables grow best in soil with a pH between 6.0 to 7.0—in other words, slightly acidic. As a rule, rainy climates have acidic soil that needs the pH raised, usually by adding lime, and arid climates have fairly neutral or alkaline soil that needs extra organic matter to lower the pH.

Once you've decided on where you are going to plant, it's time to choose your vegetables. Your major consideration is, of course, what flavors you enjoy using in the kitchen. With this in mind, look for species and varieties that grow well in your climate. As a rule, gardeners in northern climates and high elevations look for vegetables that tolerate cool or short summer conditions. Gardeners in hot, humid areas require plants that tolerate diseases well and need to consider carefully choosing heat-tolerant vegetables.

The USDA Plant Hardiness Zone Map groups eleven zones according to winter lows, a help in choosing perennial plants but of limited use for annual vegetables. Of additional interest to the vegetable gardener is the AHS Plant Heat-Zone Map, published by the American Horticultural Society. The heat map details twelve zones that indicate the average number of days each year when a given area experiences temperatures of 86°F or higher—the temperature at which many plants, including peas and most salad greens, begin to suffer physiological damage. In the "Encyclopedia of Mexican Vegetables" (page 21), I indicate which varieties have a low tolerance to high temperatures and those that grow well in hot weather. See the Bibliography for information on obtaining the heat map.

Crop placement must also be considered. Take care not to plant tall crops, such as corn, where they will shade sun-loving plants, such as peppers. Setting out a plan for crop rotation is wise at this point, too, and certainly must be considered in already established gardens. (See the "Crop Rotation" entry on page 94).

Other design features to consider include bed size, paths, and fences. A garden of a few hundred square feet, or more, needs a path or two and the soil to be arranged in beds. Paths through any garden should be at least 3 feet across to provide ample room for walking and using a wheelbarrow. Beds should generally be limited to 5 feet across, as that is the average distance a person can reach into the bed to harvest or pull weeds from both sides. Protection, too, is often needed, so consider putting a fence or wall around the garden to give it a stronger design and to keep out rabbits, woodchucks, and the resident dog. Assuming you have chosen a nice sunny area, selected a design, and determined that your soil drains properly, you are ready to prepare the soil.

Preparing the Soil

To prepare the soil for a new vegetable garden, first remove large rocks and weeds. Dig out any perennial weeds, especially grasses like Bermuda and quack grass. You need to sift and closely examine each shovelful for every little piece of their roots, or they will regrow with a vengeance. If you are taking up part of a lawn, the sod needs to be removed. If it is a small area, this can be done with a flat spade. Removing large sections, though, warrants renting a sod cutter. Next, when the soil is not too wet, spade over the area.

Most vegetables are heavy feeders and few soils support them without being supplemented with much organic matter and nutrients. The big-three nutrients are nitrogen (N), phosphorus (P), and potassium (K)—the ones most frequently found in fertilizers. Calcium, magnesium, and sulfur are also important plant nutrients, and plants need a number of trace minerals for healthy growth, among them iron, zinc, boron, copper, and manganese. A soil test is the best way to see what your soil needs. In general, most soils benefit from at least an application of an organic nitrogen fertilizer. While it's hard to say what your soil needs without a test, the following gives you a rough idea of how much you need per 100 square feet of average soil: for nitrogen, apply blood meal at 2 pounds or fish meal at 2 1/4 pounds; for phosphorus, apply 2 pounds bonemeal; for potassium, apply kelp meal according to the package or, in acidic soils, 1 1/2 pounds of wood ashes. Kelp meal also provides most trace minerals. (The addition of so many nutrients will not be needed in subsequent years if composting and mulching are practiced, especially if you rotate your crops and use cover crops.)

After the area is spaded, cover it with 4 or 5 inches of compost, 1 or 2 inches of well-aged manure, and any other needed fertilizers. Add a few more inches of compost if you live in a hot, humid climate where heat burns the compost at an acceler-ated rate, or if you have very alkaline, sandy, or heavy clay soil. (In subsequent years, an application of 2 to 3 inches of compost should be sufficient, except in the cases of the problem soils mentioned.) If a soil test indicates that your soil is too acidic, apply lime (which may be applied in the spring, but it is better to apply it in the fall so that it has more time to react with the soil before spring planting). Incorporate all the ingredients thoroughly by turning the soil over with a spade, working the amendments into the top 6 to 10 inches. (For best results, add half the nitrogen fertilizer while doing this initial bed preparation and scratch the other half into the top couple of inches of soil after the bed is prepared.) If your garden is large or the soil is very hard to work, you might use a rototiller. When you put in a garden for the first time, a rototiller can be very helpful. However, research has shown that continued use of tillers is hard on soil structure and quickly burns up valuable organic matter if used regularly.

Finally, grade and rake the area. You are now ready to form the beds and paths. Because of all the added materials, the beds will now be elevated above the paths—which further helps drainage. Slope the sides of the beds so that loose soil is not easily washed or knocked onto the paths. Some gardeners add a brick or wood edging to outline the beds. Some sort of gravel, brick, stone, or mulch is needed on the paths to forestall weed growth and to prevent your feet from getting wet and muddy.

The last task before planting your garden is providing support for vining crops, like pole beans and chayotes. There are many types of supports, from simple stakes to wooden trellises; whichever you choose, installing them before you plant is best.

Starting from Seeds

You can grow all annual vegetables from seeds. They can be started indoors in flats or other well-drained containers, outdoors in a cold frame, or, depending on the time of year, directly in the garden. When I start annual vegetables inside, I seed them either in plastic pony packs that I recycle from the nursery or in Styrofoam compartmentalized containers, variously called plugs or speedling trays (available from mail-order garden supply houses). Whatever type of container you use, the soil should be 2 to 3 inches deep. Shallower soil dries out too fast and deeper soil is usually a waste of seed-starting soil and water.

Starting seeds inside gives your seedlings a safe start away from slugs and birds. It also allows gardeners in cold or hot climates to get a jump on the season. Many vegetables can be started four to six weeks before the last expected frost date and then transplanted out into the garden as soon as the soil can be worked. Furthermore, some vegetables are sensitive to high temperatures; by starting fall crops inside in mid- or late summer, the seeds germinate and the seedlings get a good start and are ready to be transplanted outside in early fall, when the weather starts to cool.

The cultural needs of seeds vary widely among species; still, some basic rules apply to most seeding procedures. First, whether starting seeds in the ground or in a container, make sure you have loose, water-retentive soil that drains well. Good drainage is important because seeds can get waterlogged, which can lead to damping off, a fungal disease that kills seedlings at the soil line. Commercial starting mixes are usually best because they have been sterilized to remove weed seeds; however, the quality varies greatly from brand to brand and I find most lack enough nitrogen, so I water with a weak solution of fish emulsion when I plant the seeds, and again a week or so later.

Smooth the soil surface and plant the seeds at the recommended depth. Information on seed depth is included in the "Encyclopedia of Mexican Vegetables" (page 21) as well as on the back of most seed packages. Pat down the seeds and water carefully to make the seed bed moist but not soggy. Mark the name of the plant, the variety, and the date of seeding on a plastic or wooden label and place it at the head of the row. When starting seeds outside, protect the seed bed with either floating row covers or bird netting to keep out critters. If slugs and snails are a problem, circle the area with hardwood ashes or diatomaceous earth to keep them away. Go out at night with a flashlight to catch any that cross the barrier. If you are starting seeds in containers, put the seedling tray in a warm but not hot place to help seeds germinate more quickly.

When starting seeds inside, once they have germinated it's imperative that they immediately be given a high-quality source of light; otherwise, the new seedlings will be spindly and pale. A greenhouse, sun porch, or south-facing window with no overhang will suffice, provided it is warm. If such a place is not available, use fluorescent lights, which are available from home-supply stores and specialty mail-order houses. Hang the lights just above the plants for maximum light (no farther than 3 or 4 inches away, at most); move them up as the plants get taller. Another option I use, if the weather is above 60°F, is to put my seedling trays outside on a table in the sun and protect them with bird netting during the day, bringing them in at night.

Once seedlings are up, keep them moist and, if you have seeded thickly and have crowded plants, thin some out. It's less damaging to do so with small scissors. Cut the little plants out, leaving the remaining seedlings an inch or so apart. Do not transplant your seedlings until they have their second set of true leaves (the first leaves that sprout from a seed are called seed leaves and usually look different from the later true leaves). If the seedlings are tender, wait until all danger of frost is past before you set them out. In fact, don't put heat-loving melons and peppers out until the weather is thoroughly warmed up and stable. Young plants started indoors should be hardened off before they are planted in the garden—that is, they should be put outside in a sheltered place for a few days in their containers to let them get used to the differences in temperature, humidity, and air movement outside. A cold frame is perfect for hardening off plants.

Transplanting

Before setting transplants out in the garden, check to see if a mat of roots has formed at the bottom of the root ball. Remove this or open it up so the roots won't continue to grow in a tangled mass. Set the plant in the ground at the same height as it was in the container, pat the plant in place gently by hand, and water each plant in well to remove air bubbles. Space plants so that they won't be crowded once they mature; when vegetables grow too close together, they are prone to rot diseases and mildew. If

planting on a very hot day or the transplants have been in a protected greenhouse, shade them with a shingle or such placed on the sunny side of the plants. Then install irrigation ooze tubing (see "Watering and Irrigation Systems" on page 93) and mulch with a few inches of organic matter. I keep the transplants moist but not soggy for the first few weeks.

Mulching

Among the many benefits of mulching is the moderation of soil temperatures. A thick organic mulch helps keep pepper roots from getting too hot in hot-summer regions and a black plastic mulch warms soil in cool regions in preparation for transplanting. Mulching also reduces moisture loss, prevents erosion, controls weeds, and minimizes soil compaction. When the mulch is an organic material, it adds nutrients and organic matter to the soil as it decomposes, making heavy clay more porous and helping sandy soil retain moisture. Organic mulches include finished compost from your compost pile, grass clippings, pine needles, composted sawdust, straw, and one of many agricultural byproducts, like rice hulls or grape pomace. Layers of black-and-white newspaper are often used for mulching peppers in the Southwest; it is particularly good at deterring weeds, conserving moisture, and reflecting heat. The sheets of newspaper are anchored by partially covering with soil.

Like many other organic mulches, newspaper can be tilled or dug in at the end of the season. Coarse, woody mulches, such as wood and bark chips and shredded bark, do not work well as mulches in vegetable gardens as they break down slowly and take nitrogen from the soil. However, they do make good mulches for pathways or other areas of a more permanent nature.

In cooler, short-season areas, organic mulches are applied after the soil is warm. If your pepper yield is low, the mulch may be keeping your soil too cool for peppers. Use black plastic to warm the soil before planting and consider partially mulching with black plastic through the growing season. Due to its warming qualities, black plastic is not used in hot climates. When you remove plastic, dispose of it. Black plastic does not decompose, although some brands claim to; it is more likely that they degrade into small pieces rather than decompose. Various other plastic mulches, called IRT (Infra-Red Transmitting), have the heat-transmitting qualities of clear plastic. These IRT plastic mulches can be green or red and warm soil more quickly than regular black plastic; they also discourage weed growth (which clear plastic does not). IRT is available from some local garden supply stores and mail-order garden suppliers.

Mulch using black plastic

A three-bin composting system

Composting

Compost is the humus-rich result of the decomposition of organic matter, such as leaves and garden trimmings. The objective of maintaining a composting system is to speed decomposition and centralize the material so you can gather it up and spread it where it will do the most good. Compost's benefits include providing nutrients to plants in a slow-release, balanced fashion, helping break up clay soil, aiding sandy soil to retain moisture, and correcting pH problems. On top of that, compost is free, it can be made at home, and it is an excellent way to recycle our yard and kitchen wastes. Compost can be used as a soil additive or a mulch.

There need be no great mystique about composting. To create the environment needed by the decay-causing microorganisms that do all the work, just include the following four ingredients, mixed well: 3 or 4 parts brown material high in carbon, such as dry leaves, dry grass, and even shredded black-and-white newspaper; one part green material high in nitrogen, such as fresh grass clippings, fresh garden trimmings, barnyard manure, and kitchen trimmings like pea pods and carrot tops; water in moderate amounts, so that the mixture is moist but not soggy; and air to supply oxygen to the microorganisms. Bury the kitchen trimmings within the pile so as not to attract flies. Cut large pieces of material. Exclude weeds that have gone to seed and noxious perennial weeds such as Bermuda grass, because they can lead to the growth of those weeds in the garden. Do not add meat, fat, diseased plants of any kind, woody branches, or cat or dog manure.

I don't stress myself about the proper proportions of compost materials as long as I have a fairly good mix of materials from the garden. If the decomposition is too slow, it is usually because the pile has too much brown material, is too dry, or needs air. If the pile smells, there is too much green material or it is too wet. To speed decomposition, I often chop or shred the materials before adding them to the pile; I may turn the pile occasionally to increase oxygen to all parts. During decomposition, the materials can become quite hot and steamy, which is preferred; however, it is not mandatory that the compost become extremely hot.

You can make compost in a simple pile, in wire or wood bins, or in rather expensive containers. The bin's size should be about 3 feet high, wide, and deep (3 cubic feet) for the most efficient decomposition and so the pile is easily workable. It can be larger, but too much so and it becomes hard to manage. In rainy climates, it's a good idea to have a cover for the compost. I like to use three bins. I collect the compost materials in one bin, have a working bin, and, when that bin is full, I turn the contents into the last bin, where it finishes its decomposition. I sift the finished compost into empty garbage cans so it does not leach its nutrients into the soil. The empty bin is then ready to fill again.

Watering and Irrigation Systems

There is no easy formula for determining the correct amount or frequency of watering. Proper watering takes experience and observation. In addition to the specific watering needs of individual plants, the amount of watering needed depends on soil type, wind conditions, and air temperature. To water properly, you must learn how to recognize water-stress symptoms (often a dulling of foliage color as well as the better-known symptoms of drooping leaves and wilting), how much to water (too much is as bad as too little), and how to water. Some general rules are:

1. Water deeply. Except for seed beds, most plants need infrequent deep watering rather than frequent light sprinkling.

2. To ensure proper absorption, apply water at a rate slow enough to prevent runoff.

3. Do not use overhead watering systems when the wind is blowing.

4. Try to water in the morning so that foliage has time to dry off before nightfall, thus preventing some disease problems. In addition, because of the cooler temperature, less water is lost to evaporation.

5. Test your watering system occasionally to make sure it is covering the area evenly.

6. Use methods and tools that conserve water. When using a hose, use a nozzle or watering wand that shuts off the water while you move from one container or planting bed to another. Soaker hoses, made of canvas or recycled tires, and other ooze- and drip-irrigation systems apply water slowly and use water more efficiently than do overhead systems.

Drip- or the related ooze-irrigation systems are advisable wherever feasible, and most gardens are well suited to them. Drip systems deliver water a drop at a time through spaghettilike emitter tubes or plastic pipes with emitters that drip water right onto the root zone of each plant. Because of the time and effort involved in installing one or two emitters per plant, drip systems make the most sense for permanent plantings. The lines require continual maintenance to make sure the individual emitters are not clogged.

Similar systems, called ooze systems, deliver water through holes made every 6 or 12 inches along solid flexible tubing or ooze along an entirely porous hose. Both of these systems work well in vegetable gardens. Neither is as prone to clogging as are drip emitters. The solid type is made of plastic and is often called laser tubing. It is pressure compensated, which means the flow of water is even throughout the length of the tubing. The high-quality brands feature a built-in mechanism to minimize clogging and are made of tubing that does not expand in hot weather and, consequently, pop off its fittings. (Some of the inexpensive drip-irrigation kits can make you crazy!) The porous hose types are made from recycled tires and come in two sizes—a standard hose diameter of 1 inch, great for shrubs and trees planted in a row, and $\frac{1}{2}$-inch tubing that can be snaked around beds of small plants. Neither are pressure compensated, which means the plants nearest the source of water get more water than those at the end of the line. It also means they do not work well if the land slopes.

All types of drip-emitter and ooze systems are installed after the plants or seeds are in the ground and are held in place with ground staples. To install these systems, you must also install an antisiphon valve at the water source to prevent dirty garden water from being drawn up into the house's drinking water. Further, a filter is needed to prevent debris from clogging the emitters. To set up the system, 1-inch distribution tubing is connected to the water source and laid out around the perimeter of the garden. Then smaller-diameter drip and ooze lines are connected to this. As you can see, installing these systems requires some thought and time. You can order these systems from a specialty mail-order garden or irrigation source or visit your local plumbing-store. I find the latter to be the best solution for all my irrigation problems. Over the years, I've found that plumbing-supply stores offer professional-quality supplies, usually for less money than the so-called inexpensive kits available in home-supply stores and some nurseries. In addition to excellent materials, plumbing-store professionals can help you lay out an irrigation design that is tailored to your garden.

Whether you choose an emitter or an ooze system, when you go to buy your tubing, be prepared by bringing a rough drawing of the area to be irrigated—with dimensions, the location of the water source and any slopes, and, if possible, the water pressure at your water source. Let the professionals walk you through the steps and help pick out supplies that best fit your site.

Problems aside, all forms of drip and ooze irrigation are more efficient than furrow or standard overhead watering in delivering water to its precise destination and are well worth considering. They deliver water slowly, so it doesn't run off; they also water deeply, which encourages deep rooting. They also eliminate many disease problems and, because so little of the soil surface is moist, there are fewer weeds. Finally, they have the potential to waste a lot less water.

Weeding

Weeding is needed to make sure unwanted plants don't compete with and overpower your vegetables and herbs. A small triangular hoe will help you weed a small garden if you start when the weeds are young and easily hoed. If you allow the weeds to get large, a session of hand pulling is needed. Be cautious, as many plants are shallow rooted. Applying a mulch is a great way to cut down on weeds; however, if you have a big problem with slugs in your garden, the mulch gives them more places to hide. Another means of controlling weeds, especially annual weeds, like crabgrass, is a new organic preemergence herbicide made from corn gluten called Concern Weed Prevention Plus. This gluten meal inhibits the tiny feeder roots of germinating weed seeds, so they wither and die. It does not kill existing weeds. Obviously, if you use it among new seedlings or in seed beds, it kills them too, so it is only useful in areas away from very young plants.

Crop Rotation

Rotating crops in an edible garden has been practiced for centuries. The object is to avoid growing members of the same family in the same spot year after year, as related plants are often prone to the same diseases and pests and deplete the same nutrients. For example, peppers should not follow eggplants or tomatoes, as all are Solanaceae family plants and all are prone to fusarium wilt. On the other hand, in southeastern gardens, quick-growing cabbage family plants, such as mustard, make a great crop to rotate with peppers, as they discourage the root knot nematodes to which many peppers are susceptible.

Crop rotation is also practiced to help keep the soil nutrient level up. The pea family (legumes), which includes not only peas and beans but also clovers and alfalfa, adds nitrogen to the soil. In contrast, most members of the cabbage, cucumber, and tomato families deplete the soil of nitrogen. Because most vegetables deplete the soil, knowledgeable gardeners not only rotate their beds with vegetables from different families, they also include an occasional cover crop of clover or other legume and other soil benefactors, such as buckwheat. After growing for a few months, these crops are turned under, providing organic matter and many nutrients. Some cover crops (like rye) are grown over the winter to control soil erosion. The seeds of all sorts of cover crops are available from farm suppliers and specialty seed companies.

The following is a short list of related vegetables and herbs. The plants listed for each family are not comprehensive; they are examples of the type of plants in that family.

Apiaceae (parsley or carrot family)—includes carrots, celeriac, celery, chervil, coriander (cilantro), dill, fennel, lovage, parsley, parsnips

Asteraceae (sunflower or daisy family, also called composites)—includes artichokes, calendulas, celtuce, chicories, dandelions, endives, lettuces, marigolds, tarragon

Brassicaceae (mustard or cabbage family)—includes arugula, broccoli, cabbages, cauliflower, collards, cresses, kale, kohlrabi, komatsuna, mizuna, mustards, radishes, turnips

Chenopodiaceae (goosefoot family)—includes beets, chard, orach, spinach

Cucurbitaceae (cucumber or gourd family)—includes cucumbers, gourds, melons, summer squash, winter squash, pumpkins

Fabaceae (pea family, also called legumes)—includes beans, cowpeas, fava beans, lima beans, peanuts, peas, runner beans, soybeans, sugar peas

Floating row cover

Lamiaceae (mint family)—includes basil, mints, oregano, rosemary, sages, summer savory, thymes

Liliaceae (lily family)—includes asparagus, chives, garlic, leeks, onions, Oriental chives, shallots

Solanaceae (nightshade or tomato family)—includes eggplants, peppers, potatoes, tomatillos, tomatoes

Floating Row Covers

Among the most valuable tools for plant protection in the vegetable garden are floating row covers made of lightweight spunbond polyester or polypropylene fabric. These are laid directly over the plants, where they "float" in place, though they can also be stretched over hoops. These covers can be used to protect plants against cold weather or to shade them in extremely hot and sunny climates. If used correctly, row covers are a most effective pest control for various beetles and caterpillars, leafhoppers, aphids, and leaf miners. The most lightweight covers, usually called summerweight or insect barriers because they generate little heat buildup, can be used throughout the season for insect control in all but the hottest and coldest climates. They cut down on 10 percent of the sunlight, which is seldom a problem unless your garden is already partly shady. Heavier versions, sometimes called garden covers under trade names including Reemay and Tufbell, variously cut down from 15 percent to 50 percent of the sunlight—which could be a problem for some plants, such as peppers—but they also raise the temperature underneath between 2°F and 7°F, which can help to protect plants from early fall frosts or to extend the season in cool-summer areas. Another way to raise the temperature is to use two layers of the lightweight cover.

Other advantages to using floating row covers include:

• The stronger ones protect plants from most songbirds, though not from crafty squirrels and blue jays.

• They raise the humidity around plants—a bonus in arid climates but a problem in humid climates.

• They protect young seedlings from sunburn in summer and in high-altitude gardens.

There are a few limitations to consider:

• These covers keep out pollinating bees (which could be a plus if you are saving seed and are concerned with cross-pollination).

• Many of the fabrics last only a year and then start to deteriorate. (I use tattered small pieces to cover containers, in the bottoms of containers to keep out slugs, etc.)

• Row covers use petroleum products and eventually end up in the landfill.

• In very windy areas, tunnels and floating row covers are apt to be blown away or become shredded.

• The heavyweight versions may cut down on too much light and are useful only to help raise temperatures when frost threatens.

Rolls of the fabric, from 5 to 10 feet wide and up to 100 feet long, can be purchased from local nurseries or ordered from garden-supply catalogs. As a rule, mail-order sources offer a wider selection of materials and sizes.

Before you apply row covers for pest protection, fully prepare the bed and make sure it's free of eggs, larvae, and adult pests. Then install drip irrigation, if you are using it, plant your crop, and mulch (if appropriate). There are two ways to lay a row cover: directly on the plants and stretched over wire hoops. Laying the cover directly on the plants is the easiest approach. However, laying it over hoops has the advantage of being easier to check under, and some plants are sensitive to abrasion if the wind whips the cover around, which causes the tips of the plants to turn brown. When you lay the fiber directly on the plants, leave some slack so plants have room to grow. For both methods, secure the edges completely with bricks, rocks, old pieces of lumber, bent wire hangers, or U-shaped metal pins sold for this purpose.

To avoid pitfalls, it's critical to check under the row covers from time to time. Check soil moisture; the fibers sometimes shed rain and overhead irrigation water. Check, as well, for weeds; the protective fiber aids their growth too. Most important, check for insect pests that may have been trapped inside.

appendix B
pest and disease control

The following sections cover a large number of pests and diseases. The individual gardener, however, encounters few such problems in a lifetime of gardening. Good garden planning, good hygiene, and an awareness of major symptoms keep problems to a minimum and give you many hours to enjoy your garden and feast on its bounty.

There are some spoilers, though, which sometimes need control. For years, controls were presented as a list of critters and diseases, followed by the newest and best chemical to control them. But times have changed, and we now know that chasing the latest chemical to fortify our arsenal is a bit like chasing our tail. That's because most pesticides, both insecticides and fungicides, kill beneficial insects as well as the pests; therefore, the more we spray, the more we are forced to spray. Nowadays, we've learned that successful pest control focuses on prevention, plus beefing up the natural ecosystem so beneficial insects are on pest patrol. How does that translate to pest control for the vegetable garden directly?

1. When possible, seek varieties that are resistant to pests and diseases.

2. Use mechanical means to prevent insect pests from damaging the plants. For example, cover radishes with floating row covers to keep away flea beetles and imported cabbageworm; sprinkle wood ashes around plants to prevent slug damage; put cardboard collars around young pepper and tomato seedlings to prevent cutworms from destroying them.

3. Clean up diseased foliage and dispose of it in the garbage to cut down on the cycle of infection.

4. Rotate your crops so that plants from the same family are not planted in the same place for two consecutive seasons. (See "Crop Rotation," page 94.)

5. Encourage and provide food for beneficial insects. In the vegetable garden, this translates to letting a few selected vegetables go to flower and growing flowering herbs and ornamentals to provide a season-long source of nectar and pollen for beneficial insects.

Beneficial Insects

In a nutshell, few insects are potential problems; most are either neutral or beneficial to the gardener. Given the chance, the beneficials do much of your insect control for you, provided that you don't use pesticides, which are apt to kill them as well as the problem insects. Like predatory lions stalking zebra, predatory ladybugs (lady beetles) and lacewing larvae hunt and eat aphids that might be attracted to your beans, say. Or say a miniwasp parasitoid lays eggs in the aphids. If you spray those aphids, even with a so-called benign pesticide such as insecticidal soap or pyrethrum, you'll kill off those ladybugs and lacewings and that baby parasitoid wasp, too. Most insecticides are broad spectrum, which means that they kill insects indiscriminately, not just the pests. In my opinion, organic gardeners who regularly use organic broad-spectrum insecticides have missed this point. While it is true they are using an "organic" pesticide, they may actually be eliminating a truly organic means of control, the beneficial insects.

Unfortunately, many gardeners are not aware of the benefits of the predator-prey relationship and are not able to recognize beneficial insects. The following sections will help you identify both helpful and pest organisms. A more detailed aid for identifying insects is *Rodale's Color Handbook of Garden Insects,* by Anna Carr. A hand lens is an invaluable and inexpensive tool that will also help you identify the insects in your garden.

Predators and Parasitoids

Insects that feed on other insects are divided into two types: predators and parasitoids. Predators are mobile. They stalk plants looking for such plant feeders as aphids and mites. Parasitoids, on the other hand, are insects that develop in or on the bodies, pupae, or eggs of other host insects. Most parasitoids are minute wasps or flies whose larvae (young stages) eat other insects from within. Some of the wasps are so small they can develop within an aphid or an insect egg. One parasitoid egg can divide into several identical cells, each developing into identical miniwasp larvae, which then can kill an entire caterpillar. Though nearly invisible to most gardeners, parasitoids are the most specific and effective means of insect control.

The predator-prey relationship can be a fairly stable situation; when the natural system is working properly, pest insects inhabiting the garden along with the predators and parasitoids seldom become a problem. Sometimes, though, the system breaks down. For example, a number of imported pests have taken hold in this country, and unfortunately, their natural predators did not accompany them. Four pesky examples are Japanese beetles, the European brown snail, the white cabbage butterfly, and flea beetles. None of these organisms has natural enemies in this country that provide sufficient control. Where they occur, it is sometimes necessary to use physical means or selective pesticides that kill only the problem insect.

Weather extremes sometime produce imbalances as well. For example, long stretches of hot, dry weather favor grasshoppers that invade vegetable gardens, because the diseases that keep them in check are more prevalent under moist conditions. Predator-prey relationships also get out of balance because gardening practices often inadvertently work in favor of the pests. For example, when gardeners spray with broad-spectrum pesticides regularly, not all the insects in the garden are killed—and because predators and parasitoids generally reproduce more slowly than do the pests, regular spraying usually tips the balance in favor of the pest populations. Further, all too often the average yard has few plants that produce nectar for beneficial insects; instead, it is filled with grass and shrubs, so that when a few vegetables are put in, the new plants attract the aphids but not the beneficials. Being aware of the effect of these practices will help you create a vegetable garden that is relatively free of many pest problems.

Attracting Beneficial Insects

Besides reducing your use of pesticides, the key to keeping a healthy balance in your garden is providing a diversity of plants, including plenty that produce nectar and pollen. Nectar is the primary food of the adult stage and some larval stages of many beneficial insects. Interplanting your vegetables with flowers and numerous herbs helps

attract them. Ornamentals, like species zinnias, marigolds, alyssum, and yarrow, provide many flowers over a long season and are shallow enough for insects to reach the nectar. Large, dense flowers like tea roses and dahlias offer little, as their nectar is out of reach. A number of the herbs are rich nectar sources, including cilantro, fennel, dill, anise, all the oreganos, thyme, and parsley. Allowing a few of your herbs and vegetables, like lettuce and radishes, go to flower is helpful because their tiny flowers, full of nectar and pollen, are just what many of the beneficial insects need.

Following are a few of the predatory and parasitoid insects helpful in the garden. Their preservation and protection should be a major goal of your pest-control strategy.

Ground beetles and their larvae are all predators. Most adult ground beetles are fairly large black beetles that scurry out from under plants or containers when you disturb them. Their favorite foods are soft-bodied larvae like cutworms and root maggots (root maggots eat cabbage-family plants); some ground beetles even eat snails and slugs. If supplied with an undisturbed place to live, like your compost area or groupings of perennial plantings, ground beetles will be long-lived residents of your garden.

Lacewings are one of the most effective insect predators in the home garden. They are small green or brown gossamer-winged insects that, in their adult stage, eat flower nectar, pollen, aphid honeydew, and sometimes aphids and mealybugs. In the larval stage, they look like little tan alligators. Called aphid lions, the larvae are fierce predators of aphids, mites, and whiteflies—all occasional pests that suck plant sap. If you are having problems with sucking insects in your garden, consider purchasing lacewing eggs or larvae

via mail order to jump-start your lacewing population. Remember to plant lots of nectar plants to keep the population going from year to year.

Lady beetles (ladybugs) are the best known of the beneficial garden insects. Actually, there are about four hundred species of lady beetles in North America alone. They come in a variety of colors and markings in addition to the familiar red with black spots, but they are never green. Lady beetles and their fierce-looking alligator-shaped larvae eat copious amounts of aphids and other small insects.

Spiders are close relatives of insects. The hundreds of spider species are some of the most effective predators of a great range of pest insects.

Syrphid flies (also called flower flies and hover flies) look like very small bees hovering over flowers, but they have only two wings. Many have yellow and black stripes on their body. Their larvae are small green maggots that inhabit leaves and eat aphids, other small sucking insects, and mites.

Wasps are a large family of insects with transparent wings. Unfortunately, the few large wasps that sting have given all wasps a bad name. In fact, all wasps are either insect predators or parasitoids. The miniwasps are usually parasitoids; the adult female lays her eggs in such insects as aphids, whitefly larvae, and caterpillars—and the developing wasp larvae devour the host. These miniature wasps are also available for purchase from insectaries and are especially effective when released in greenhouses.

Pests

The following pests are sometimes a problem in the vegetable garden.

Aphids are soft-bodied, small, green, black, pink, or gray insects that produce many generations in one season. They suck plant juices and exude honeydew.

Sometimes leaves under the aphids turn black from a mold growing on the nutrient-rich honeydew. Aphids are particularly attracted to cabbage-family plants, beans, and peas.

Aphid populations can build up, especially in the spring, before beneficial insects are present in large numbers and when plants are covered by row covers or are growing in cold frames. The presence of aphids sometimes indicates that the plant is under stress—perhaps the cabbage isn't getting enough water and sunlight. Check first to see if stress is a problem and then try to correct it. Look also for aphid mummies and other natural enemies mentioned above. Mummies are swollen brown or metallic-looking aphids. Inside the mummy, a wasp parasitoid is growing. They are valuable, so keep them. To remove aphids generally, wash the foliage with a strong blast of water and cut back the foliage if they persist. Fertilize and water the plant and check on it in a few days. Repeat with the water spray a few more times. In extreme situations, spray with insecticidal soap or a neem product.

A number of **beetles** are garden pests, including Mexican bean beetles, cucumber beetles, flea beetles, and wireworms (the larvae of click beetles). All are a problem throughout most of North America. Colorado potato beetles and Japanese beetles are primarily a problem in the eastern United States. Mexican bean beetles look like brown lady beetles with oval black spots; as their name implies, they feed on beans. Cucumber beetles are ladybuglike green or yellow green beetles with black stripes or spots. Their larvae feed on the roots of corn and other vegetables. The adults devour members of the cucumber family, corn tassels, beans, and some salad greens. Flea beetles are minuscule black and white striped beetles hardly big enough to be seen. The grubs feed on the roots and lower leaves of many vegetables and the adults chew on the leaves of eggplants, radishes, peppers, and other plants, causing the leaves to look shot full of tiny holes. The adult click beetle is rarely seen, and its

young, a brown, inch-long, shiny larva called a wireworm, works underground and damages tubers, seeds, and roots. Colorado potato beetles are larger and rounder than lady beetles and have red brown heads and black and yellow-striped backs. Adults and larvae eat the leaves of eggplants and peppers as well as other plants in the Solanaceae family, so crop rotation with another plant family is essential if Colorado potato beetles are a problem in your area. Japanese beetles are fairly large metallic blue or green beetles with coppery wings. The larval stage (a white grub) lives on the roots of grasses; the adult skeletonizes leaves and chews flowers and buds of beans and many other plants.

The larger beetles, if not present in great numbers, can be controlled by hand picking—in the morning is best, when the beetles are slower. Knock them into a bowl or bucket of soapy water. Flea beetles are too small to gather by hand; try a handheld vacuum instead. Insecticidal soap on the underside of the leaves is also effective on flea beetles. Wireworms can be trapped by putting cut pieces of potatoes or carrots every 5 feet or so in the soil and then digging them up after a few days. Destroy the worms.

Because many beetle species winter over in the soil, crop rotation and fall cleanup is vital. Polyester row covers securely fastened to the ground can provide excellent control for most beetles if used in combination with crop rotation. Obviously, row covers are of no use if the beetles are in a larval stage and ready to emerge from the soil under the row cover or if the adults are already established on the plant. Row covers also have limited use on plants (such as squashes and melons) that need bees to pollinate the blooms, as bees also are excluded.

New evidence indicates that beneficial nematodes are effective in controlling most pest beetles if applied during the beetles' soil-dwelling larval stage. Colorado potato beetles can also be controlled, when very young, by applications of *Bacillus thuringiensis* var. *san diego,* a beetle Bt that has proven effective for flea beetles as well. Azadirachtin (the active ingredient in some formulations of neem) is also effective against the immature stage of most beetles and can act as a feeding deterrent for adults. Japanese beetle populations can also be

reduced by applications of milky-spore, a naturally occurring soil-borne disease that infects the beetle in its grub stage—though the disease is slow to work. The grubs primarily feed in lawns; the application of lime, if your lawn is acidic, has been reported to help control grubs, too.

Caterpillars (sometimes called loopers or worms) are the immature stage of moths and butterflies. Most pose no problem in our gardens and we encourage them to visit, but a few are a problem in the vegetable garden. Among the most notorious are the beanloopers, cutworms, and the numerous cabbage worms and loopers that chew ragged holes in leaves. Natural controls include birds, wasps, and disease. Encourage birds by providing a birdbath, shelter, and berry-producing shrubs. Tolerate wasp nests if they're not a threat and provide nectar plants for the miniwasps. Hand picking is effective as well. The disease *Bacillus thuringiensis* var. *kurstaki* is available as a spray in a number of formulations. Brands include Bt kurstaki, Dipel, and Thuricide. This is a bacteria that, if applied when the caterpillar is fairly young, causes it to starve to death. Bt-k Bait contains the disease and lures budworms away from vegetables and to it. I seldom use Bt in any form, as it also kills all butterfly and harmless moth larvae.

Cutworms are the caterpillar stage of various moth species. They are usually found in the soil and curl up into a ball when disturbed. Cutworms are a particular problem on annual vegetables when the seedlings first appear and when young transplants are set out. The cutworm often chews off the stem right at the soil line, killing the plant. Control cutworms by using cardboard collars or bottomless tin cans around the plant stem; be sure to sink these collars 1 inch into the ground. *Bacillus thuringiensis* gives limited control. Trichogramma miniwasps and black ground beetles are among cutworms' natural enemies, but they are often not present in a new garden.

Leaf miners tunnel through leaves, disfiguring them by causing patches of dead tissue where they feed; they do not burrow into the roots. Leaf miners are the larvae of a small fly and can be controlled somewhat by neem or by applying beneficial nematodes.

Mites are among the few arachnids (spiders and their kin) that pose a problem. Mites are so small that a hand lens is usually needed to see them. They become a problem when they reproduce in great numbers. A symptom of serious mite damage is stippling on the leaves in the form of tiny white or yellow  spots, sometimes accompanied by tiny webs. The major natural predators of pest mites are predatory mites, mite-eating thrips, and syrphid flies.

Mites are most likely to thrive on dusty leaves and in warm weather. A routine foliage wash and misting of sensitive vegetables helps control them. Mites are seldom a serious problem unless heavy-duty pesticides that kill off predatory mites have been used or plants are grown in the house. Cut back the plants and, if you're using heavy-duty pesticides, stop the applications, and the balance could return. If all else fails, use the neem derivative, Green Light Fruit, Nut, and Vegetable Spray, or dispose of the plant.

Nematodes are microscopic round worms that inhabit the soil in most of the United States, particularly in the Southeast. Most nematode species live on decaying matter or are predatory on other nematodes, insects, or bacteria. A few types are parasitic, attaching themselves to the roots of plants. Edible plants particularly susceptible to nematode damage include beans, melons, peppers, tomatoes, and some perennial herbs. The symptoms of nematode damage are stunted-looking plants and small swellings or lesions on the roots.

Rotate annual vegetables with less susceptible varieties, plant contaminated beds with a blanket of marigolds for a whole season, and keep your soil high in organic matter (to encourage fungi and predatory nematodes, both of which act as biological controls). If all else fails, grow edibles in containers with sterilized soil.

Snails and slugs are not insects, of course, but mollusks. They are especially fond of greens and seedlings of most vegetables. They feed at night and can go dormant for months in times of stress. In the absence of effective natural enemies (a few snail eggs are consumed by predatory beetles and earwigs), several snail-control strategies can be recommended. Because snails and slugs are most active after rain or irrigation, go out and destroy them on such nights. Only repeated forays provide adequate control. Hardwood ashes dusted around susceptible plants give some control. Planter boxes with a strip of copper applied along the top perimeter boards effectively keep slugs and snails out; they won't cross the barrier. A word of warning: overhanging leaves that can provide a bridge into the bed will defeat the barrier. New organic slug and snail baits made with chelated iron as the active ingredient, Sluggo and Escar-Go!, show promise. When the snails and slugs consume the bait, they stop eating and eventually die. As with any bait or pesticide, it is best not to use these regularly.

Thrips are tiny, hard-to-see, torpedo-shaped insects that can be a problem on many plants, including onions and peas. The damage they do can be quite noticeable. Leaf-feeding thrips leave a silvery sheen and flecks of discoloration on the leaf surface. To control, keep plants adequately watered, as the predators of thrips live in the moist soil around the plants. If necessary, spot-treat infected areas with insecticidal soap.

Whiteflies are sometimes a problem in mild-winter areas of the country as well as in greenhouses nationwide. Susceptible crops include beans and tomatoes. Whiteflies can be a persistent problem if plants are against a building or fence where air circulation is limited. In the garden, Encarsia wasps and other parasitoids usually provide adequate whitefly control. Occasionally, especially in cool weather or in greenhouses, whitefly populations may begin to cause serious plant damage (wilting and slowed growth or flowering). Look under the leaves to determine whether the scalelike immobile larvae, the young crawling stage, or the pupae are present in large numbers. If so, wash them off with water from your hose. Repeat the washing three days in a row. In addition, try vacuuming up the adults with a handheld vacuum early in the day while the weather is still cool and they are less active. Insecticidal soap sprays can be effective as well.

Wildlife Problems

Rabbits and mice can cause problems for gardeners. To keep them out, use fine-weave fencing around the vegetable garden. If gophers or moles are a problem, plant large vegetables, such as peppers, in chicken wire baskets in the ground. Make the wire stick up a foot from the ground so the critters can't reach inside. In severe situations, you might have to line whole beds with chicken wire. Gophers usually need to be trapped. Trapping for moles is less successful, but repellents like MoleMed sometimes help. Cats help with all rodent problems but seldom provide adequate control. Small, portable electric fences help keep raccoons, squirrels, and woodchucks out of the garden. Small-diameter wire mesh, bent into boxes and anchored with ground staples, protects seedlings from squirrels and chipmunks.

Deer are a serious problem—they love vegetables. I've tried myriad repellents, but they gave only short-term control. In some areas, deer cause such severe problems that edible plants can't be grown without tall electric or nine-foot fences and/or an aggressive dog. The exception is herbs, deer don't feed on most culinary herbs.

Songbirds, starlings, and crows can be major pests of young seedlings, particularly corn and lettuce. Cover the emerging plants with bird netting and firmly anchor it to the ground so birds can't get under it and feast.

Pest Controls

Insecticidal soap sprays are effective against many pest insects, including caterpillars, aphids, mites, and whiteflies. They can be purchased, or you can make a soap spray at home. As a rule, I recommend purchasing insecticidal soaps because they are carefully formulated to give the most effective control and are less apt to burn your vegetables. If you do make your own, use a mild liquid dishwashing soap, not caustic detergents.

Neem-based pesticide and fungicide products, which are derived from the neem tree (*Azadirachta indica*), have relatively low toxicity to mammals but are effective against a wide range of insects. Neem products are considered organic pesticides by some organizations but not by others.

Products containing azadirachtin, a derivative of neem, are affective because azadirachtin is an insect growth regulator that affects the ability of immature stages of insects such as leaf miners, cucumber beetles, and aphids to develop to adulthood. BioNeem and Azatin are commercial pesticides containing azadirachtin. Another neem product, Green Light Fruit, Nut, and Vegetable Spray™, contains clarified hydrophobic extract of neem oil and is effective against mites, aphids, and some fungus diseases. Neem products are still fairly new in the United States. Although neem was at first thought to be harmless to beneficial insects, some studies now show that some parasitoid beneficial insects that feed on neem-treated pest insects were unable to survive to adulthood.

Pyrethrum, a botanical insecticide, is toxic to a wide range of insects but has relatively low toxicity to most mammals and breaks down quickly. The active ingredients in pyrethrum are pyrethrins derived from chrysanthemum flowers. Do not confuse pyrethrum with pyrethoids, which are much more toxic synthetics that do not biodegrade as quickly. Many pyrethrums have a synergist, piperonyl butoxide (PBO), added to increase effectiveness. As there is evidence that PBO may affect the human nervous system, try to use pyrethrums without this ingredient. Wear gloves, goggles, and a respirator when using any pyrethrum.

Diseases

Plant diseases are potentially far more damaging to your vegetables than are most insects. There are two types of diseases: those caused by nutrient deficiencies and those caused by pathogens. Diseases caused by pathogens, such as root rots, are difficult to control once they begin. Therefore, most plant disease control strategies feature prevention rather than cure.

To keep diseases under control, it is very important to plant the right plant in the right place. For instance, root rots (such as that caused by phytophthora) can be a problem for Mexican oregano and peppers if planted in poorly drained soil. Check the cultural needs of a plant before placing it in your garden. Proper light, air circulation, temperature, fertilization, and moisture are important factors in disease control. Finally, whenever possible, choose disease-resistant varieties when a particular pathogen is present or when conditions are optimal for the disease. The entries for individual plants in the "Encyclopedia of Mexican Vegetables" give specific cultural and variety information. As a final note, plants infected with disease pathogens should always be discarded, not composted.

Nutritional Deficiencies

For more basic information on plant nutrients, see the soil preparation information given in Appendix A (page 90). As with pathogens, the best way to solve nutritional problems is to prevent them. While mineral deficiencies do affect vegetables, most often caused by a pH that is below 6 or above 7.5, the most common nutritional deficiency is a lack of nitrogen. Vegetables need fairly high amounts of nitrogen in the soil to keep growing vigorously. Nitrogen deficiency is especially prevalent in sandy soil and in soil low in organic matter. The main symptom of nitrogen deficiency is a pale and slightly yellow cast to the foliage, especially the lower, older leaves. To correct the problem, supplement your beds with a good source of organic nitrogen, like blood meal or chicken manure. For most vegetables, as they are going to be growing for a long season, additional side dressings of a liquid nitrogen, such as fish emulsion, may be needed monthly or bimonthly.

While I've stressed nitrogen deficiency, the real trick is to reach a good nitrogen balance in your soil; although plants must have nitrogen to grow, too much causes leaf edges to die, promotes succulent new growth savored by aphids, and makes plants prone to cold damage.

Diseases Caused by Pathogens

Anthracnose is a fungus that is primarily a problem in the eastern United States on beans, tomatoes, cucumbers, and melons. Affected plants develop spots on the leaves; furthermore, beans develop sunken black spots on the pods and stems, and melons, cucumbers, and tomatoes develop sunken spots on the fruits. The disease spreads readily in wet weather and overwinters in the soil on debris. Crop rotation, good air circulation, and choosing resistant varieties are the best defenses. Neem-based Green Light Fruit, Nut, and Vegetable Spray™ gives some control.

A number of fungi and bacteria affect vegetables and their names hint at the damage they do—blights, wilts, and leaf spots. As a rule, they are more of a problem in rainy and humid areas. Given the right conditions, they can be a problem in most of North America. Bacterial wilt affects cucumbers, melons, and, sometimes, squash. The disease is spread by cucumber beetles and causes the plants to wilt and eventually die. To diagnose the disease, cut a wilted stem and look for milky sap that forms a thread when the tip of a stick touches it and is drawn away. The disease overwinters in cucumber beetles; cutting their population and installing floating row covers over young plants are the best defenses.

Damping off is caused by a parasitic fungus that lives near the soil surface and attacks young plants in their early seedling stage. It causes them to wilt and fall over just where they emerge from the soil. This fungus thrives under dark, humid conditions, so it can often be thwarted by keeping the seedlings in fast-draining soil in a bright, well-ventilated place. In addition, when possible, start seedlings in sterilized soil.

Fusarium wilt is a soil-borne fungus most prevalent in the warm parts of the country. It causes an overall wilting of the plant visible as the leaves from the base of the plant upward yellow and die. The plants most susceptible to strains of the disease include peppers, tomatoes, squash, melons, peas, and basil. While a serious problem in some areas, this disease can be controlled by planting only resistant varieties. Crop rotation is also helpful.

Mildews are fungal diseases that affect some vegetables—particularly peas, melons, and squash—under certain conditions. There are two types of mildews: powdery and downy. Powdery mildew appears as a white powdery dust on the surface; downy mildew makes velvety or fuzzy white, yellow, or purple patches on leaves, buds, and tender stems. The poorer the air circulation and more humid the weather, the more apt your plants are to have downy mildew. For both mildews, make sure the plants have plenty of sun and are not crowded by other vegetation. If you must use overhead watering, do it in the morning. In some cases, powdery mildew can be washed off the plant. Do so early in the day so that the plant has time to dry before evening. Powdery mildew is almost always present at the end of the season on squash and pea plants but is not a problem because they are usually through producing.

Lightweight summer horticultural oil combined with baking soda has proved effective against powdery mildew on some plants in research at Cornell University. Combine 1 tablespoon baking soda and 2 $\frac{1}{2}$ teaspoons summer oil with 1 gallon of water. Spray weekly. Test on a small part of the plant first. Don't use horticultural oil on very hot days or on plants that are moisture-stressed; after applying the oil, wait at least a month before using any sulfur sprays on the same plant.

A tea for combating powdery mildew and, possibly, other disease-causing fungi can be made by wrapping a gallon of well-aged manure-based compost in burlap and steeping it in a five-gallon bucket of water for about three days in a warm place. Spray every three to four days, in the evening, if possible, until symptoms disappear.

Root rots and crown rots are caused by a number of fungi. The classic symptom of root rot is wilting—even when a plant is well watered. Sometimes one side of the plant wilts but, more often, the whole plant wilts. Affected plants are often stunted and yellow as well. The diagnosis is complete when the dead plant is pulled up to reveal rotten, black roots. Crown rot is a fungus that kills plants at the crown; it is primarily a problem in the Northeast. Root and crown rots are most often caused by poor drainage. There is no cure for root and crown rots once they involve the whole plant. Remove and destroy the plants and correct the drainage problem.

Verticillium wilt is a soil-borne fungus that can be a problem in most of North America, especially the cooler sections. The symptom of this disease is a sudden wilting of one part of or all of the plant. If you continually lose tomatoes or eggplants, this, or one of the other wilts, could be the problem. There is no cure, so plant resistant species or varieties if this disease is in your soil.

Viruses attack a number of plants. Symptoms are stunted growth and deformed or mottled leaves. The mosaic viruses destroy chlorophyll in the leaves, causing them to become yellow and blotched in a mosaic pattern. There is no cure for viral conditions, so the affected plants must be destroyed. Cucumbers and beans are particularly susceptible. In the Northwest, pea enation mosaic virus is a problem. Viral diseases can be transmitted by aphids and leaf hoppers and by seeds, so seed savers should be extra careful to learn the symptoms in individual plant species. When available, use resistant varieties.

resources

Seeds and Plants

Abundant Life Seed Foundation
P.O. Box 772
Port Townsend, WA 98368
$2.00 donation for catalog; nonprofit organization specializing in open-pollinated, heirloom, and endangered seeds; Membership: $30.00, Limited income: $20.00

Bountiful Gardens
18001 Shafer Ranch Road
Willits, CA 95490-9626
Catalog free in USA, $2.00 outside of USA; carries open-pollinated seeds and organic gardening supplies

W. Atlee Burpee Company
Warminster, PA 18974
Vegetable, herb, and flower seeds

Chiltern Seeds
Bortree Stile
Ulverston
Cumbria LA12 7PB
England
Large variety of seeds, including Opuntia ficus-indica, jícama, tomatillos, purslane, cilantro, cumin, and epazote

Corns
Route 1, Box 32
Turpin, OK 73950
$3.00 donation for seed list; organization working to preserve the genetic diversity of open-pollinated corn varieties

ECHO
Educational Concerns for Hunger
Organization
17430 Durrance Road
North Fort Myers, FL 33917
Nonprofit organization specializing in seeds of underused edible tropical plants; carries amaranth, 'Pozole' corn, virus-free tepary beans, jícama, roselle

Enchanted Seeds
P.O. Box 6087
Las Cruces, NM 88006
Extensive selection of peppers

Filaree Farms
182 Conconully Highway
Okanogan, WA 98840
$2.00 for catalog; specializes in organically grown garlic

Fox Hollow Seeds
P.O. Box 148
McGrann, PA 16236
$1.00 for catalog; heirloom herbs, vegetables, flowers

Garden Medicinals and Culinaries
P.O. Box 320
Earlysville, VA 22936
$2.00 for catalog; herb seeds and plants

Goodwin Creek Gardens
P.O. Box 83
Williams, OR 97544
Wide selection of herbs and nursery-propagated native plants, including plants of Opuntia humifusa

Horticultural Enterprises
P.O. Box 810082
Dallas, TX 75381-0082
Specializes in peppers; ships only to USA

Hurov's Seeds & Botanicals
P.O. Box 1596
Chula Vista, CA 91912
$1.00 for catalog; seeds of over 6,000 species from around the world; specializes in useful plants, including rare herbs and tropical fruits and vegetables; carries Opuntia cacti

J. L. Hudson, Seedsman
Star Route 2, Box 337
La Honda, CA 94020
For catalog:
P.O. Box 1058
Redwood City, CA 94064
$1.00 for catalog; wide selection of seeds, including many hard-to-find varieties

Johnny's Selected Seeds
Foss Hill Road
Albion, ME 04910
Excellent selection of herb and vegetable seeds; unusual varieties

Lockhart Seeds
3 North Wilson Way
P.O. Box 1361
Stockton, CA 95201

Native Seeds/SEARCH
526 North Fourth Avenue
Tucson, AZ 85705
$1.00 for catalog for nonmembers; nonprofit organization dedicated to preservation of tradi-

tional crops, seeds, and farming methods of the native peoples of southwest USA and northern Mexico; Membership: $20.00, Low income/student: $12.00; membership includes quarterly newsletter and catalog

Nichols Garden Nursery
1190 North Pacific Highway NE
Albany, OR 97321-4580
Superior varieties of vegetables, herbs, and flowers

The Pepper Gal
P.O. Box 23006
Fort Lauderdale, FL 33307-3006
$2.00 for catalog; wide selection of peppers

Pinetree Garden Seeds
Box 300
New Gloucester, ME 04260
Carries Mexican vegetables and herbs in the catalog's Latin American and Native American sections

Plantasia Cactus Gardens
867 Filer Avenue W
Twin Falls, ID 83301
Specializes in winter-hardy cacti

Plants of the Southwest
Agua Fria, Route 6, Box 11A
Santa Fe, NM 87501
$3.50 for catalog; open-pollinated seeds of warmth-loving vegetables

Redwood City Seed Company
P.O. Box 361
Redwood City, CA 94064
www.ecoseeds.com
$1.00 for catalog in USA, Canada, Mexico; $2.00 to other countries; specializes in endangered cultivated plants; carries many vegetables and herbs used in Mexican cuisine

Richters Herbs
357 Highway 47
Goodwood, Ontario
Canada L0C 1A0
Extensive selection of herb seeds and plants, as well as some unusual vegetables

Seeds of Change
P.O. Box 15700
Santa Fe, NM 87506
Seeds of many unusual Mexican vegetables, including heirlooms; selected garden tools

Seed Savers Exchange
3076 North Winn Road
Decorah, IA 52101
Catalog for selected seeds free to nonmembers and members; nonprofit organization dedicated to saving vegetable gene-pool diversity; the only source for many rare and heirloom vegetable seeds; members join an extensive network of gardeners saving and exchanging seeds; Membership fee: $25.00, Low income/senior/student: $20.00, Canadian: $30.00, Overseas: $40.00

Shepherd's Garden Seeds
30 Irene Street
Torrington, CT 06790
Excellent varieties of vegetables, herbs, and flowers

R. H. Shumway's
P.O. Box 1
Graniteville, SC 29829
Wide variety of seeds, including many heirlooms

Southern Exposure Seed Exchange
P.O. Box 170
Earlysville, VA 22936
$2.00 for catalog; specializes in open-pollinated, heirloom, and heat-tolerant vegetables

Stokes Seeds, Inc.
P.O. Box 548
Buffalo, NY 14240
Carries an excellent selection of vegetables for northern gardens, including many peppers

Synergy Seeds
Box 787
Somes Bar, CA 95568
$2.00 for seed list; large selection of organically grown herb, vegetable, and flower seeds, including papaloquelite and Malva crispa

Territorial Seed Company
P.O. Box 157
Cottage Grove, OR 97424-0061
Good selection of open-pollinated vegetables and herbs

Thompson & Morgan Ltd.
Poplar Lane
Ipswich
Suffolk 1P8 3BU
England
Wide variety of different types of seeds

Tomato Growers Supply Company
P.O. Box 2237
Fort Myers, FL 33902
Extensive selection of all types of tomatoes and peppers

Totally Tomatoes
P.O. Box 1626
Augusta, GA 30903
Extensive selection of all types of tomatoes and peppers

Vermont Bean Seed Company
Garden Lane
Fair Haven, VT 05743
Extensive selection of beans, plus other vegetables

Well-Sweep Herb Farm
205 Mount Bethel Road
Port Murray, NJ 07865
$2.00 for catalog; wide selection of herb seeds and plants

Willhite Seed Company, Inc.
P.O. Box 23
Poolville, TX 76487
Specializes in warm-weather crops

Gardening and Cooking Suppliers

The CMC Company
P.O. Box 322
Avalon, NJ 08202
Great selection of dried Mexican herbs and chiles and other cooking specialties; some Mexican cooking utensils

Don Alfonso Foods
P.O. Box 201988
Austin, TX 78720
A huge selection of dried Mexican herbs and chiles, canned products, cooking utensils, and Mexican cookbooks

Gardener's Supply Company
128 Intervale Road
Burlington, VT 05401
Gardening tools and supplies; particularly good selection of floating row covers

Gardens Alive!
5100 Schenley Place
Lawrenceburg, IN 47025
Carries Escar-Go! for slug and snail control, as

well as many other organic gardening products

Herbs of Mexico
3903 Whittier Boulevard
Los Angeles, California 90086
Carries most Mexican dried herbs
Native Seeds/SEARCH
526 North Fourth Avenue
Tucson, AZ 85705
*$1.00 for catalog for nonmembers;
Membership: $20.00, Low income/student:
$12.00; fascinating selection of foodstuffs,
including red and blue cornmeals, beans, chile
products, traditional southwestern herbs; membership includes 10 percent discount on items
in the catalog*

The Natural Gardening Company
217 San Anselmo Avenue
San Anselmo, CA 94960
*Gardening supplies, organic fertilizers, and
organically grown seeds and plants*

Nutrite Inc.
P.O. Box 160
Elmira, Ontario
Canada N3B 2Z6
Canadian source of gardening supplies

Peaceful Valley Farm Supply
P.O. Box 2209
Grass Valley, CA 95945
*Gardening supplies, organic fertilizers, seeds
for cover crops*

Sur la Table
Catalog Division
1765 Sixth Avenue South
Seattle, WA 98134
Cooking equipment

The Urban Farmer Store
2833 Vincente Street
San Francisco, CA 94116

Williams-Sonoma
Mail Order Department
P.O. Box 7456
San Francisco, CA 94120-7456
Cooking equipment

Wycliffe Gardens
P.O. Box 430
Kimberly, British Columbia
Canada V1A 2Y9
Canadian source of gardening supplies

Books

Ashworth, Suzanne. *Seed to Seed: Seed-
Saving Techniques for the Vegetable
Gardener.* Decorah, Iowa: Seed Saver
Publications, 1991.
*A comprehensive guide offering proven
techniques for saving the seeds from your
garden.*

Bender, Steve, editor. *Southern Living
Garden Book.* Birmingham, Ala.:
Oxmoor House, 1998.
*A great basic book for southern garden-
ing.*

Bayless, Rick, with Deann Groen Bayless.
*Authentic Mexican: Regional Cooking
from the Heart of Mexico.* New York:
William Morrow and Company, 1987.
*A real must for cooks interested in
Mexican cooking. It covers the many
complexities of the cuisine in an easy-to-
use format.*

Bubel, Nancy. *The New Seed-Starters
Handbook.* Emmaus, Pa.: Rodale Press,
1988.
*Great for gardeners interested in starting
their own seeds.*

Carr, Anna. *Rodale's Color Handbook of
Garden Insects.* Emmaus, Pa.: Rodale
Press, 1979.
*A valuable resource with color pho-
tographs to help gardeners identify benefi-
cial and pest insects.*

Cathey, Dr. H. Marc, and Linda Bellamy.
*Heat-Zone Gardening: How to Choose
Plants That Thrive in Your Region's
Warmest Weather.* Alexandria, Va.:
Time-Life Books, 1998.
*Finally, a book that addresses the issue of
plant heat tolerance (or intolerance);
shows how to use the AHS Heat-Zone
Map and, while it includes few vegetables, it covers the general concepts and
limitations of too much or too little heat
in the garden, a valuable aid in growing
many Mexican plants.*

Editors of Sunset Books and Sunset magazine. *Sunset National Garden Book.*
Menlo Park, Calif.: Sunset Books,
1997.
*Encyclopedia of botanical and growing
information for over 6,000 plants.*

—. *Sunset Western Garden Book.* Menlo
Park, Calif.: Sunset Publishing, 1995.
*Long considered the gardening bible for
western gardeners, this is the western ver-*

sion of the Sunset National Garden Book.

Facciola, Stephen. *Cornucopia II: A Source
Book for Edible Plants.* Vista, Calif.:
Kampong Publications, 1998.
*An incredibly rich resource, this is an
encyclopedia of over 3,000 species of edible plants and up-to-date sources for all
of them.*

Cutler, Karan Davis. *Burpee: The Complete
Vegetable and Herb Gardener: A Guide
to Growing Your Garden Organically.*
New York: Macmillan, 1997.
*Wonderful new guide to gardening
organically.*

DeWitt, Dave, and Paul W. Bosland. *How
to Grow Peppers: The Pepper Garden—
From the Sweetest Bells to the Hottest
Habañero.* New York: Macmillan,
1997.
*Reliable advice for pepper gardening with
attention to the requirements of each of
the five main cultivated species.*

—. *Peppers of the World: An Identification
Guide.* Berkeley: Ten Speed Press,
1996.
*Thorough research and beautiful pho-
tographs by DeWitt and Bosland make
this a must-have guide for pepper lovers.*

Gilkeson, Linda, Pam Peirce, and Miranda
Smith. *Rodale's Pest and Disease
Problem Solver: A Chemical-Free Guide
to Keeping Your Garden Healthy.*
Emmaus, Pa.: Rodale Press, 1996.
*Good color photographs of beneficial and
pest insects, along with lots of sensible
advice.*

Hutson, Lucinda. *The Herb Garden
Cookbook,* 2nd edition. Houston, TX:
Gulf Publishing, 1998.
*Lots of great recipes for the gardener,
including much information on Mexican
herbs.*

Kennedy, Diana. *The Art of Mexican
Cooking: Traditional Mexican Cooking
for Aficionados.* New York: Bantam
Books, 1989.
*This is one of the definitive texts on
Mexican cooking, a must for your library.*

—. *The Cuisines of Mexico.* New York:
Harper Collins, 1989 (revised edition)

—. *Mexican Regional Cooking.* New York:
Harper & Row, 1984.
*Here Diana Kennedy explores many
recipes from all over Mexico.*

—. *My Mexico: A Culinary Odyssey with
More than 300 Recipes.* New York:

Clarkson Potter, 1998.
Yet more authentic exciting Mexican recipes from Diana Kennedy.

Nabhan, Gary Paul. *Gathering the Desert.* Tucson: University of Arizona Press, 1985.
Gary Paul's books are a wonderful blend of meticulous ethnobotanical and ecological research, desert adventures, and philosophical prose, applicable here because much of his research has been in Mexico.

Olkowski, William, Sheila Daar, and Helga Olkowski. *The Gardener's Guide to Common-Sense Pest Control.* Newtown, Conn.: Taunton Press, 1995.
Thoroughly researched information on pest control for the home gardener.

Pleasant, Barbara. *The Gardener's Bug Book: Earth-Safe Insect Control.* Pownal, Vt.: Storey Communications, 1994.
Up-to-date information combined with time-tested remedies that are safe for the gardener and the beneficial insects.

—. *The Gardener's Guide to Plant Diseases: Earth-Safe Remedies.* Pownal, Vt.: Storey Communications, 1995.
Another gem from Barbara Pleasant, with safe techniques for prevention as well as control of diseases.

Saville, Carole. *Exotic Herbs.* New York: Henry Holt, 1997.
Superb growing and culinary advice spiced with fascinating herb history from one of today's most knowledgeable herb mavens.

Schildreff, Marjorie, and Clyde Schildreff, editors. *Adventures in Mexican Cooking.* San Francisco: Ortho Books, 1978.
This comprehensive book on Mexican cooking is filled with photos and is particularly helpful in explaining how ingredients from the garden are used.

Whealy, Kent, editor. *The Garden Seed Inventory,* 5th edition. Decorah, Iowa.: Seed Savers Exchange, 1999.
This valuable book lists all nonhybrid vegetable seeds available in the USA and Canada and their mail-order sources.

Urdaneta, Maria Luisa, Ph.D. and Daryle F. Kanter, RN. *Deleites de la Cocina Mexicana: Healthy Mexican American Cooking.* Austin, Tex.: University of Texas Press, 1996.
A helpful book for folks who want to cut down on the fat in traditional Mexican cooking. Has lots of great recipes.

Zaslavsky, Nancy. *A Cook's Tour of Mexico: Authentic Recipes from the Country's Best Open-Air Markets, City Fondas, and Home Kitchens.* New York: St. Martin's Griffin, 1995.
No trip to Mexico should be taken without this book. For the cook at home, it includes many great authentic recipes.

—. *Meatless Mexican Home Cooking.* New York: St. Martin's Griffin, 1999.

Magazines

The Kitchen Garden. The Taunton Press, 63 Main St., P.O. Box 5506, Newtown, CT 06470.
A magazine that covers many aspects of garden cooking, including an occasional story on the foods of Mexico.

Other Resources

American Horticulture Society. "Plant Heat-Zone Map." 1-800-777-7931, Extension 45. Cost: $15.00.

Chile Pepper Institute
New Mexico State University
Box 30003, Department 3Q
Las Cruces, NM 88003-8003
Phone: 505-646-3028
email: hotchile@nmsu.edu
Web site: www.nmsu.edu/~hotchile
Membership: $25.00; includes quarterly newsletter, membership directory, occasional seed samples; recipes and other publications available. Call or e-mail if you have questions about growing peppers.

acknowledgments

My garden is the foundation for my books, photography, and recipes. For nearly twelve months of the year, we toil to keep it beautiful, bountiful, and organic! Unlike most gardens, as it is a photo studio and trial plot, my garden must look glorious, be healthy, and produce for the kitchen in every season. Needless to say, this is a large undertaking. For two decades, a quartet of talented organic gardener/cooks have not only given the garden hundreds of hours of loving attention but also they have been generous with their vast knowledge of plants. Together we have forged our concept of gardening and cooking, much of which I share with you in this series of garden cookbooks.

I wish to thank Wendy Krupnick for giving the garden such a strong foundation and Joe Queirolo for maintaining it for many years. For the last decade, Jody Main and Duncan Minalga have helped me to greatly expand my garden horizons. No matter how complex the project, they enthusiastically rise to the occasion. In the kitchen, I am most fortunate to have Gudi Riter, a gifted cook and food lover. I thank her for the help she provides as we create recipes and present them in all their glory.

I thank Dayna Lane for her steady hand and editorial assistance. In addition to day-to-day compilations, she joins me on our constant search for the most effective organic pest controls, superior varieties, and the best sources for plants.

A book such as this needs much technical support. Diana Kennedy's help was invaluable a decade ago when I was starting on my Mexican garden adventure; Lucinda Hutson opened her Texas garden and shared her herb and chile information, complete with a tour of the Tijuana Mercado; Olivia and Cruz Montañez, owners of the Imperial Spice Company, and Juvenal Chavez, owner of Mi Pueblo markets in San José, gave hours of detailed plant and cooking details; Jeff Dawson, then Garden Director at Kendall Jackson Vineyards, opened his vast chile and Mexican plantings to me; Ed Walsh and Tess McDonough, chefs at the Kendall Jackson Winery, and Virginia Torres gave me recipes. Luis Torres, cooking maven, expanded my basic knowledge of Mexican recipes and cooking ingredients and provided a number of recipes.

Gardeners and cooking professionals are by nature most generous. I want to thank Carole Saville, who helped across the board with recipe ideas and photo safaris, and who contributed much of the information on Mexican herbs; Craig Dremann of the Redwood City Seed Company, for hours of plant identification and sleuthing; and Nancy Zaslavsky, for generously sharing her vast knowledge of Mexican cooking and many recipe ideas.

I would also like to thank a large supporting cast: especially my daughter Laura and my extended Mexican-American family, including her husband, Joel Chavarin, ever ready for a trip to the Mexican market and to clarify basic cooking concepts; Rachel, Chris, Veronica, and Alex Chavarin, who help and encourage; my daughter-in-law, Julie Creasy, who is always ready to try Mexican recipes with my son, Bob; and my husband, Robert, who gives such high-quality technical advice and loving support.

Many people were instrumental in bringing this book project to fruition. They include Jane Whitfield, Linda Gunnarson, and David Humphrey, who were integral to the initial vision; Kathryn Sky-Peck, who provided the style and quality of the layout; and Marcy Hawthorne, who made the lovely drawings. Heartfelt thanks to Eric Oey and to the entire Periplus staff, especially Deane Norton and Jan Johnson, for their help. Finally, I would like to thank my editor, Jeanine Caunt, for her strong presence, many talents, and dedication to quality.